The Demon of Writing

The Demon of Writing

Powers and Failures of Paperwork

Ben Kafka

ZONE BOOKS · NEW YORK

2012

ZONE BOOKS
1226 Prospect Avenue
Brooklyn, NY 11218

Printed in the United States of America.

Distributed by The MIT Press,
Cambridge, Massachusetts, and London, England

Library of Congress Cataloging-in-Publication Data

Kafka, Ben.
    The demon of writing: powers and failures of
powerwork / Ben Kafka.
        p. cm.
    Includes bibliographical references and index.
    ISBN 978-1-935408-26-0 (alk. paper)
    1. Public records—History. 2. Government paper-
work—History. I. Title.

JF1521.K34 2012
342'0662—dc23

                              2012024897

Contents

Not perverts but bureaucrats will set things off, and we won't even know if their intentions were good or bad.
—Jacques Lacan, *Seminar VII: The Ethics of Psychoanalysis* (1959–1960)

The Psychic Life of Paperwork

The management of the modern office is based upon written documents (the "files"), which are preserved in their original or draft form, and upon a staff of subaltern officials and scribes of all sorts.
—Max Weber, *Economy and Society* (1922)

Bentham's Panopticon, Weber's Iron Cage, Kafka's Castle—since the beginning of the modern era, these buildings have darkened our skyline. Even as the crowds were tearing down the Bastille, that monument to tyranny, officials were busy erecting still more formidable institutions from which to tax and spend, protect and serve, discipline and punish. Shut your eyes for a moment and summon up images of the interiors: the waiting rooms, hallways, doorways, and offices where clerks sit writing, copying, calculating, or staring off into space. Memos, forms, files, registers spilling out of desks, drawers, shelves, cabinets.

This book is about paperwork and its contradictions. It begins with the observation that notwithstanding its reputation for tedium, paperwork is full of surprises. The ballot that is supposed to serve as the foundation of representative government is spoiled by a dimpled chad. The tax form that is supposed to ensure that we all share the costs of government turns out to be incomprehensible to all but a few. The warrant that is supposed to protect against arbitrary search and seizure is mistakenly written for the wrong address. The visa that is supposed to help us work or travel keeps us returning to the same place over and over again, hoping, this time, that we remembered to bring the right supporting documents. And these are only the most visible kinds of records—the "charismatic megafauna" of paperwork. Behind each of these are hundreds or thousands or hundreds of thousands more opportunities to misspell a word, miscalculate a number, misread a blank, misunderstand an instruction, misaddress an envelope. Paperwork syncopates the state's rhythms, destabilizes its structures. Under ordinary conditions, the mishaps are corrected, rhythms restored, structures restabilized. But under extraordinary conditions—war, revolution, natural disaster—even the most minor technical error can have catastrophic results.

I take "paperwork" to mean all those documents produced in response to a demand—real or imagined—by the state. This includes everything from sums recorded by lowly clerks, to petitions submitted by indignant citizens, to founding declarations maintained by official archivists in climate-controlled repositories. In its tersest form, my argument is that paperwork is unpredictable and that this unpredictability is frustrating: it frustrates those of us who write memos or fill out forms as part of our jobs; it frustrates those of us who need a stamp or signature to get on with our lives; and, above all, it frustrates the intellect, including the intellects of the intellectuals.

Indeed, as I will argue in this book, modern political thought was both founded and confounded by its encounters with paperwork. Instead of a critical theory of the "bureaucratic medium," a term Marx used once in passing, we have a myth, or a collection of myths, about bureaucracy and bureaucrats. There is a strange consistency to these myths, that is to say, it is strange how consistent they are, and the consistency itself is strange—easy to grasp, but hard to get a grip on. The anthropologist Michael Herzfeld, drawing on fieldwork in Greece, refers to the stories we tell each other about bureaucracy as "secular theodicies," that is to say, efforts to explain, and sometimes to explain away, the existence

of incompetence, indifference, or corruption of political institutions.[1] We tend to condemn bureaucracy and bureaucrats when
better explanations elude us. There is an old saying that a myth
is the imaginative or imaginary resolution of real contradictions;
the myths of bureaucracy seek not only to resolve paperwork's
contradictions, but also the contradictions in our own thought.
We have been unable to reconcile our theories of the state's
power with our experience of its failure.

This project was originally inspired by my rather literal-minded
reading of Jacques Derrida's *Of Grammatology*. For Derrida, philosophy has always preferred speech to writing, which it regards
with suspicion as a "fallen, secondary, instituted" form of communication.[2] What is true of philosophy in general, I reasoned,
must also be true of political philosophy or political theory in
particular, which has always preferred the voice of power over its
written traces, the great discourses of kings and legislators over
the obscure scrivenings of functionaries and clerks.

I initially thought that the history of the idea of "bureaucracy"
(*la bureaucratie, die Bürokratie*) would make for a nice case study.
There is no trace of the idea in Montesquieu, Voltaire, Hume,
Rousseau, Burke, or even Hegel. Yet by the 1850s it was all the
rage. Marx's *Eighteenth Brumaire of Louis Bonaparte*, Tocqueville's
The Old Regime and the Revolution, Mill's *On Liberty*—each took a
turn denouncing bureaucracy and its agents in remarkably similar terms. What accounted for the idea's success? I attempted to
answer this question in a mode of intellectual history modeled
a bit on Michel Foucault, a bit on François Furet, and a bit on
Quentin Skinner. Following their examples, I traced the history
of the idea from its Enlightenment origins into revolutionary
journalism, postrevolutionary popular culture, and nineteenth-
century political theory.

As time passed, however, I found myself less interested in the
history of discourses about paperwork and more interested in the

stuff itself. Turning to the field of book history, I started studying paperwork's tools and techniques. The printing revolution
that transformed early modern Europe's churches, universities,
laboratories, and cafés largely bypassed its government offices. In
the French Revolution, where this book opens, clerks were still
producing and reproducing documents in much the same way as
medieval monks, using feathers plucked from geese to apply inks
derived from gall nuts to surfaces made from soiled rags or animal
skins. The manual labor required to transform these raw materials into files, registers, and finally power itself was slow, hard,
and prone to error. Split quills ruined important reports, spilt ink
delayed urgent communiqués. The development of wood-based
paper, synthetic inks, and metal nibs in the nineteenth century
may well have reduced the incidence of such mishaps, but could
never eliminate them entirely. Nibs still break. Ink still smudges.
Handwriting still cramps. Signifiers still slip. And then, even if
a piece of paper carries legible, meaningful writing, even if that
writing conveys accurate information intelligible to sender and
addressee, the message itself can easily be lost or delayed, or it can
arrive at the right place at the right time only to be mishandled
or misunderstood. Most mistakes are not the result of bad faith
or even sloppiness. They are simple, but ineluctable failures to
communicate—a literal-minded version of Derridean *différance*.

This book, thus conceived, would have had a little bit of everything that I liked most in historiography: the sophistication of
deconstruction, the erudition of intellectual history, the rigors of
book history. Or the rigors of deconstruction, the sophistication of
intellectual history, the erudition of book history. The erudition of
deconstruction, the rigors of intellectual history, the sophistication
of book history. My plan was to pick and choose methods as appropriate and then tie them neatly together with a few good microhis-
tories and the occasional dialectical deus ex machina. Whenever
anybody asked me about my methods, I told them I was "eclectic."

Then, in 2005, Joan W. Scott published an article entitled,
simply, "Against Eclecticism." She pointed to an "increasingly

evident tendency among scholars who know they have been influenced by poststructuralist theory to minimize that critical influence, to describe it as simply one among many 'methodologies' that has been used to advance empirical projects that are now taken to be the primary object of research and writing." Drawing a parallel to Victor Cousin's "philosophical eclecticism," she argued that such a strategy evades its critical responsibility. "Eclecticism," she wrote, "connotes the coexistence of conflicting doctrines as if there were no conflict, as if one position were not an explicit critique of another. The aim is to ignore or overlook differences, to create balance and harmony, to close down the opening to unknown futures that (what came to be called) 'theory' offered some twenty or thirty years ago."[3] Scott's point, it should be stressed, is not that we should embrace some theoretical, even critical-theoretical orthodoxy; she readily acknowledges that her own work has drawn on a number of theoretical sources that are at odds with one another. Rather, she objected to easy, feel-good solutions to our theoretical difficulties. So much for my hermeneutic circle around the campfire.

The book was rekindled by two texts that I discovered only after I had taken up a position as the in-house historian in a media studies department: Cornelia Vismann's *Files: Law and Media Technology* and Bruno Latour's *The Making of Law: An Ethnography of the Conseil d'État*. Vismann, a lawyer and scholar trained in the DDR, relied on the syncretic, idiosyncratic media theory of Friedrich Kittler to offer a diachronic account of the relationship between law and technologies of writing from ancient Rome to the present. Latour, well known for his contributions to science studies, presented a synchronic account of how paperwork circulated within France's highest legal institution. "Every case, at least in our country of written law, has for its corporeal envelope a cardboard cover held together by rubber bands," Latour writes. The task is to "set aside vague propositions on rights, laws, and norms in exchange for a meticulous investigation into dossiers—grey, beige, or yellow; fat or thin; simple or complicated; old or new—to see where they lead us."[4]

I have written about these and other studies of paperwork at greater length elsewhere.[5] Here let me just say that both Vismann's media archaeology and Latour's media ethnography provide elegant, intelligent, and witty—that is to say, extremely seductive—examples of what used to be called "theoretical antihumanism." But something about Latour's work, in particular, left me unpersuaded. Or rather, it persuaded me that no matter how closely I examined paperwork itself, no matter how much I learned about its materiality, I was never going to come around to the argument that things have agency like people do. This is not because I am especially sentimental about the humanity of humans, though it can be one of their nicer features. Nor do I have much patience for the idea that scholars have an obligation to "grant agency" to their subjects, an imperative that, however well-intentioned, involves a fairly serious category mistake. Rather, for reasons personal and professional, I am committed to the idea that people are ruled by unconscious processes, which is simply not true of even the most "agentic" things. Barbara Johnson has said something smart about this difference and its implications for scholarship. "The more I thought about the asymptotic relation between things and persons," she reflects in the prologue to her book *People and Things*, "the more I realized that the problem is not, as it seems, a desire to treat things as persons, but a difficulty in being sure we treat persons as persons."[6]

Our experience of paperwork's contradictions is an experience of carelessness, sometimes our own, sometimes somebody else's. Again and again, this carelessness is conflated with uncaring. "The state is the coldest of all cold monsters," writes Nietzsche.[7] "The rule by Nobody, which is what the political form known as bureaucracy is," adds Arendt.[8] This book sets out to demystify this experience and the comic-paranoid style of political thought to which it has given rise. What do we want from our paperwork? What depends on it? Who depends on it? How do we ensure its success? How do we prepare for its failure? How do we respond when these failures occur? What sorts of solidarity do we show, what sorts of resistance do we enact, what sorts of reforms do we demand? What sorts of explanations do we offer, what sorts of anecdotes do we share, what sorts of ridicule do we heap on that man or woman on the other side of the desk or telephone?

In the end, I have come to define my object of study as the psychic life of paperwork. The phrase owes something to Judith Butler ("the psychic life of power") and something else to Lydia Liu ("the psychic life of media").[9] Most of all, it owes something to my theoretical and clinical work in psychoanalysis. I would like to add a brief word about this.

One of Freud's contemporaries, the Oxford anthropologist R. R. Marret, described the psychoanalyst's excursions into history and anthropology as a collection of "just-so stories." It was not intended as a compliment, but Freud rather liked it.[10] He may not have always known what he was doing, but he usually knew when he didn't. "Our psychological analysis does not suffice even with those who are near us in space and time unless we can make them the object of years of the closest investigation," he wrote in a letter to Lytton Strachey in 1928. "With regard to the people of past times we are in the same position as with dreams to which we have been given no associations—and only a layman could expect us to interpret dreams such as those."[11]

Of course, by the time he wrote this letter, Freud had already analyzed such people of past times as Leonardo da Vinci, Daniel Paul Schreber, and Christopher Haitzmann, not to mention the primal hordes. And his sense of his own amateurishness did not prevent him from publishing *Civilization and its Discontents* the very next year. The best works of historically minded psycho-analysis or psychoanalytically minded history share this "must go on—can't go on—I'll go on" sensibility. Here, again, I turn to Joan Scott, whose emphasis on the "incommensurability of psychoanalysis and history" belongs to this tradition. For Scott, incommensurability is not an obstacle to interpretation, but an incitement to it. Psychoanalysis calls into question the concepts, categories, and narrative techniques that historians have tended to take for granted; Scott's recent work on fantasy is a powerful example of how we might transform historical practice through critical self-reflexivity.[12]

That said, this book tries a somewhat different approach to renewing and reinvigorating psychohistory. I take it as a given that our encounters with paperwork and the people who handle it inevitably reactivate some of our earliest wishes, conflicts, and fantasies about maternal provision, paternal authority, sibling rivalry, or whichever other familial division of labor happened to be in place in our childhoods. I also take it as a given that these fantasies, or at least their unconscious determinants, are inaccessible to historians—which does not mean they are of no interest, only that this interest is bound to be disappointed. Far from being evidence of the incommensurability of psychoanalysis and history, however, this should be treated as an opportunity for them to commiserate, and, yes, commensurate. Recognition of the impossibility of direct, unmediated access to the unconscious is not something that separates the two disciplines, but something that unites them. Psychoanalysis may be a science of the unconscious, but it is a practice of the *preconscious*, that intermediary region in Freud's topography of the mind where truly unconscious wishes, conflicts, and fantasies are bound up to more or less highly organized thoughts, feelings, and eventually—especially—words. To put it another way, the preconscious is where everything specific to the subject comes into contact with everything nonspecific to it. From *The Interpretation of Dreams* to *An Outline of Psychoanalysis*, Freud insisted on the importance of preconscious mediation to psychoanalytic theory and technique.[13]

Sometimes explicitly, but for the most part implicitly, this book takes the preconscious—"that chattering by means of which we articulate ourselves inside ourselves," as Lacan puts it—as its privileged level of interpretation.[14] We cannot stop ourselves from chattering about paperwork. If we listen carefully enough, I believe we will find that this chatter makes sense, that is to say, it is explicable and is itself a form of explication. Responding to this chatter, Jean-Marie Roland, who served as minister of the interior during one of the most difficult periods of the French Revolution, complained that his critics "assume that I have a lot of power because I have a lot to do."[15] The complaint is self-pitying, self-deluded, and profoundly insightful. Having a lot to do does not always mean having a lot of power, but having a lot of power always means having a lot to do, and in the modern era, at least, most of what it has to do is paperwork. The investigation of the psychic life of paperwork must be able to account for how this medium makes everyone, no matter how powerful they may be in reality, feel so powerless.

As should be clear by now, *The Demon of Writing* is not intended to overturn Weber, Tilly, Foucault, or any other "master narrative" of state formation. Nor will it substitute for smaller-scale or shorter-*durée* histories of the social, institutional, and technological aspects of paperwork (the introduction of the typewriter, the feminization of clerical labor . . .) or its genres (memoranda, petitions, government surveys, financial instruments, diplomatic correspondence, forensic records, identity documents . . .). Nor will it replace histories of information (collection, classification, visualization, overload . . .) or archivization (preservation, memorialization, destruction . . .). My hope, more modest, is that this book might take its place on a shelf alongside some of these studies.

Four chapters. In Chapter 1, I suggest that the French Revolution invented a new ethos of paperwork. In Chapter 2, I examine how paperwork worked for and against the national-security state in a time of war; this chapter also includes a first attempt at explaining paperwork's mythopoetic potentials. Chapter 3 continues this inquiry into the material and psychic realities of paperwork by following the history of the word "bureaucracy" as it emerged in the eighteenth and nineteenth centuries. The final chapter turns to Marx, Freud, and Barthes to outline a theory of paperwork that is attentive to both praxis and parapraxis. I conclude with some very brief thoughts about paperwork's future.

CHAPTER ONE

The Disciplined State

Edme-Etienne Morizot lost his job in the Ministry of Finance in September 1788. His supervisors told him that financial troubles were forcing cuts across the administration, including the Lottery Bureau, where he had been employed as a clerk for over a decade. They promised him a pension in recognition of his many years of service to the king and wished him well. He packed up his things and left.

It was all a lie. The monarchy was in plenty of trouble, but his job had not been eliminated—he had simply been replaced. Within days, somebody else was at his old desk, performing his old duties. Morizot angrily approached the controller-general of finances to appeal his termination. Upon being questioned, the supervisors confessed that yes, they had lied, but they had their reasons: Morizot was impossible to get along with. They had seized on the ministry's cost-cutting plan as a pretext to rid themselves of a troublesome employee. They reasoned that that was in fact the generous thing to do, since it entitled the clerk to a pension, which he might have lost if they had resorted to disciplinary action. The controller-general reported this back to Morizot, along with the suggestion that that he take up the matter with the director-general of finances, Jacques Necker, arguably the most powerful official in the kingdom. He turned down the clerk's request for a loan.

Out of work, out of money, out of sorts, Morizot decided to sue his former employer. But when he went to warn his supervisors, he was told that the controller-general had got it all wrong.

Sure they liked him—everyone did. They had fought to save his job. But in the end, they had been unable to protect him from enemies, powerful enemies, high up in the ministry. Indeed, the young man who replaced him was none other than the son-in-law of the king's aunt's chambermaid. Could that be a coincidence? Morizot's suspicions seemed to be confirmed when the committee set up to arbitrate the dispute dissolved after complaining that Morizot was harassing them. This, at least, was the official explanation. Morizot suspected that his enemies must have threatened them. He wrote letters to the families of the director-general, the controller-general, and various other well-placed members of the nobility—including the Princesse de Lamballe, whose mutilated corpse would later become a symbol of the Revolution's excesses—recounting his problems and asking that they exert some of their considerable influence on his behalf. He received polite responses, but no help.

As it happens, this was not the first time Morizot had suffered a setback. He had started off his professional life as a lawyer, making his way through the heavily regulated guild system to obtain the privilege of arguing cases in front of the Paris Parlement, the most powerful court in the nation. He had abandoned this path to join the Finance Ministry in 1776 under the patronage of de Clugny, the controller-general at the time, expecting a rapid rise through the ministry's ranks. But his patron's death after only six months in office had left him stranded as a lowly clerk ever since. To this humiliation was added the fact that after a period of inactivity, he had lost the right to argue cases, which he found out at the worst possible moment, having shown up at court one day to sue his brother-in-law over an inheritance. This led to a new round of litigation against the courts, which he also lost, despite having been defended by Ambroise Falconnet, one of the Old Regime's celebrity litigators.[1]

Still, his efforts were not completely wasted. The fight over his exclusion from the guild had taught him how to pursue his claims by appealing to the will of the king, the justice of the courts, the opinion of the public, and the influence of the well-connected—those well-worn paths of power traversing the political culture of the eighteenth century.[2] He knew his way around the reception rooms of the ministries, courts, and salons; he knew whom to ask for favors and how to ask for them. He had every reason, in other words, to expect that he would be able to recover his position in the Finance Ministry from the son-in-law of the king's aunt's chambermaid. He failed miserably.

The story of this failure is the story of the French Revolution's success. It is the story of a transformation in the culture of paperwork, a transformation that would have permanent consequences for modernity. This chapter sets out to follow what I have come to believe is the most important feature of this transformation, the emergence of a radical new ethics of paperwork, one designed to sustain a state whose legitimacy was founded on the claim to represent, at every moment, every member of the nation. This ethics found its most direct expression in Article 15 of the Declaration of the Rights of Man and Citizen of 1789, which established historically unprecedented guarantees of political and administrative accountability. Henceforward, every action or transaction undertaken by any person with or on behalf of the state would have to be documented in anticipation of an eventual public accounting. The disciplinary state, which relied on documents and details to keep track of its subjects, would also have to be a disciplined state, aware that those same documents and details could be used to keep track of it. For Morizot, and no doubt for many others, the sensation must have been uncanny, disorienting, terrifying. The facades of government buildings, the faces of the men who worked in them, even the documents they worked with looked very much the same as they had only months earlier. Yet they were no longer quite themselves.

"The National Assembly Doesn't Give a Damn"

Walter Benjamin tells us that certain images capture the "dialectic at a standstill";[3] this is surely the case for a series of ink drawings contributed by the great illustrator Gabriel de Saint-Aubin to a 1749 manuscript on police reform. Written by a restless gendarme named Guillaute, the treatise presented a proposal for a comprehensive system of urban surveillance that would use preprinted forms to register the name, age, address, birthplace, travels, employment history, rent due, and tax status of every resident and visitor in the city. Alert to the technical obstacles to managing so much paperwork, he also proposed a machine for storing and retrieving these forms in a rapid, reliable, and efficient manner: vertical wheels twelve feet in diameter would rotate to reveal horizontal shelves full of files (figures 1 and 2). The clerks would access these storage devices from wall terminals, controlling them with foot pedals. Each one would be able to hold more than one hundred thousand of Guillaute's forms.[4]

One of many paperwork technologies dreamed up in the eighteenth century, Guillaute's invention looked backward to Agostino Ramelli's humanist book wheel (figure 3) and still more strikingly forward to the information-storage systems employed by East Germany's state security services.[5] Saint-Aubin seems to have worked hard to integrate this posthumanist, protoindustrial paperwork machine into an idealized rococo office environment. He added Bourbon flourishes above the terminals and organic embellishments along the chair frames—standard features of what Leora Auslander, in her study of French furniture, labels absolutism's "courtly stylistic regime."[6] What makes Saint-Aubin's images so revealing, however, is not their success, either as art or as technical illustration, but their failure. The disruptive potential of the new mechanisms is not quite contained by the aristocratic social relations that Saint-Aubin so carefully encoded in the office's bright, airy aesthetic. The heavy wheels appear to be on the verge of crushing the fragile space and the order that it represents. Saint-Aubin shows us absolutism and its agents caught in the contradiction between the forces and relations of state-sponsored document production, reproduction, and exchange.

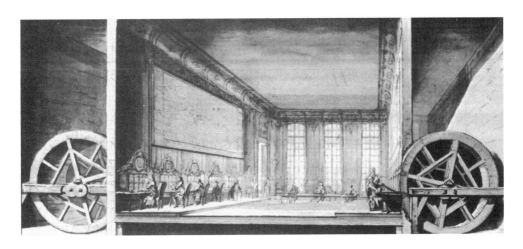

Figures 1–2. The paperwork machine from Guillauté's *Mémoire sur la réformation de la police de France* (1749).

Figure 3. The book wheel from Agostino Ramelli's *Le Diverse et artifiose machine* (1588).

An enterprising individual such as Morizot must have been familiar with both poles of this contradiction. As a clerk in the Finance Ministry, he would have encountered some of the most advanced financial and administrative instruments then available in Europe. The Lottery Bureau where he was employed was part of a sophisticated apparatus put in motion by Necker, the Swiss banker and French finance minister, to forestall royal bankruptcy through a combination of short-term and long-term loans and other fiscal measures that have come to earn the admiration of economic historians.[7] When it came time to appeal for help, however, Morizot turned to another kind of ratiocination, one based not on the new forces of production, but on aristocratic social forms. Its variables were determined by relations of privilege and patronage, influence and estate. Everyone from the peasants of French Canada to the princes of the blood performed these calculations, factoring in local customs and precedents that were themselves subject to constant variation and contestation. None of these calculations, it should be emphasized, were especially abstract, even if they required considerable sophistication to get right. Power was experienced as intensely, intimately personal. This was the central characteristic of what Thomas Ertman calls the Old Regime's "patrimonial absolutism."[8]

Holding the contradiction together with less and less success was Louis XVI, whose will alone was supposed to be absolute and universal. And so on June 14, 1789, Morizot travelled from Paris to Versailles to petition for royal justice in person. He came prepared with a memoir to distribute to the king, as well as to various ministers and delegates to the Estates General who had assembled to resolve, or not, France's political and social crises. The king formally received Morizot's memoir in a royal session on June 18, the day after the Third Estate reconstituted itself as the National Assembly, claiming for itself the right to represent the nation. The king referred the affair back to Necker, who promised to meet with Morizot that very afternoon.

At the meeting, Necker seemed distracted, anxious. Oblivious to any drama other than his own, Morizot suspected that the minister was trying to hide something from him. Necker's promise to investigate the matter further as he hurried on to more important matters only increased the clerk's rage. The next day, before returning to Paris, Morizot chanced upon Villedeuil, the minister of the royal household, and told him the whole sordid tale, confiding that he was so exasperated that he sometimes contemplated assassinating Necker as a way of bringing the whole ordeal to an end. Villedeuil promised to intervene personally if the clerk wrote him a letter describing the situation in detail. Morizot sent the letter on July 10. Villedeuil reported the death threat to Necker.

The crowds rose up, the Bastille came down. There was no news. Still unemployed, Morizot decided that he would try appealing to the National Assembly for aid. Toward the end of 1789, he prepared a new account of his situation and submitted it to the legislative body, hoping that something might be done to alleviate his misery. The case was duly assigned to the newly formed Reports Committee. The committee met with Necker, but the results of the meeting were inconclusive. In February 1790, having heard nothing, Morizot returned to the committee, only to find that its membership had rotated and that the deputies who had been initially charged with his case had since moved on to other legislative tasks. The new president of the Reports Committee, the Abbé Grégoire, upon consulting with his fellow committee member Prieur de la Marne, advised Morizot to pay more attention to his paperwork. He should submit a new memoir, this time in the form of a "detailed inventory of the abuses of ministerial and judicial power, detached from the objects of contestation that gave rise to these abuses." Such precisions were necessary, Grégoire explained, because "only these abuses belong to the competency of the legislative corps," while the actual "objects of contestation are outside it and belong exclusively to the domain of the judicial power."[9]

This time, Morizot's case was assigned to a deputy named Ricard de Sealt, a lawyer and merchant from the port city of Toulon, who, it so happens, was an acquaintance of Necker's.[10] Still nothing happened. Ricard blamed Grégoire for the delay. Grégoire blamed Ricard, who, he wrote to Morizot, had been skipping committee meetings and, most importantly, had not yet submitted a complete report on the case. Grégoire finally persuaded Ricard to meet with Lambert, but the latter denied responsibility and referred the deputy back to Necker. Morizot wrote letters to Sieyès, Robespierre, Camus, Target, and a half-dozen other deputies pleading them to intervene on his behalf, but as with the nobles whom he had entreated a year earlier, he received only encouragement. None of his correspondents seemed to be in a position to help him out.

After a few more weeks, Morizot returned to speak with Ricard. The report was still not finished. Ricard suggested that the clerk hire a writer to summarize his case as clearly and simply as possible, which he could then present to the other members of the committee as his own work. Though Morizot complied, another two months passed without the committee deliberating on his case. Meanwhile, the tension mounted. "The National Assembly doesn't give a damn," Morizot claimed to have been told by Ricard.

> I have seen another unfortunate like you, who, like you, solicited for a year, and who, like you, went twenty-one months without bread. Out of desperation, he has just opened his veins with a razor. So be it! What does that do to the National Assembly? It doesn't give a damn. Do you want to blow your brains out? The National Assembly still doesn't give a damn. What are you going to do to it? What does it have to fear?[11]

Without Ricard's report, the committee could not deliberate, let alone close the case. So it languished.

In May 1790, one of the members of the Reports Committee decided that the case would be better handled by the committee that was working to reimburse the offices and privileges that had been abolished on the night of August 4, 1789.[12] When Morizot went to the committee's office to verify that all his supporting documents were in order for the transfer, he discovered to his horror that the most important one, an irreplaceable seven-page manuscript, had gone missing. Apparently Ricard had taken it home with him and never returned it. Morizot wrote a furious letter to the deputies warning that "the committee would be wise not to permit one of its members to abuse citizens in this way. It is possible that the people will be a thousand times more tyrannized by their representatives than they were before by the officers of the king. A regime so violent can not last very long."[13] As Morizot predicted, the other committee claimed that the affair was outside its jurisdiction and returned the relevant documents to the Reports Committee.

To make matters still worse, when the president of the committee went to retrieve the memoir from Ricard as Morizot had requested, he found that it had been incinerated. It was unclear why. On July 3, 1790, a deputy named Digoine, a former marquis who, like Morizot, came from Burgundy, raised this issue in the National Assembly. "I request the floor for an unfortunate citizen oppressed by the judicial and ministerial powers," he began. "Monsieur Morizot, in whose favor I have come to claim your justice, has submitted three memoirs, pleading to receive payments for twelve years consecrated to the service of the administration, without being paid, and pleading about the minister of finances, who took away his estate for no reason." Ignoring a call to order, Digoine proceeded to describe how Morizot had been "tossed from committee to committee."[14] Then came the destruction of his papers. Digoine blamed Beaumetz, former president of the National Assembly, for allowing such confusion to reign inside the legislative committees.

Beaumetz would have none of it. "Among the large number of people who came to meet me while I was president, there was Morizot, who claimed that the administrator of the lottery owed him a large sum; he complained of abuses of judicial and ministerial powers. This affair appeared to me to be of such a nature as to be sent to the Reports Committee," he said. He continued by explaining, patiently, that since the membership of this committee was so often renewed, "an affair that concerns only a single individual can find itself deferred." There was another factor as well: "It is worth observing that Monsieur Morizot is one of the least agreeable solicitors to receive at one's home: fortunately, I do not intimidate easily. As for me, I ended up by shutting the door on him."[15] With regard to Digoine's charge that Ricard had bungled, then burned Morizot's report, Beaumetz maintained that the report had been just fine, adding, cryptically, that its destruction had taken place by arrangement between Ricard and Morizot.

Beaumetz concluded by suggesting that the whole affair be transferred to the Investigations Committee, which was responsible for police matters. Somebody else spoke up in support of this move, describing how in one meeting with Morizot the clerk had pulled out a pistol, held it to his own head, and threatened to "blow his brains out" if he did not receive justice. "Society must not include men of this type," the speaker concluded. Digoine agreed to have the case transferred to the Investigations Committee, and the National Assembly moved on to the next item on its agenda.[16] All of the speakers were presumably unaware that the Investigations Committee, at Lafayette's request, was already having Morizot followed as a potential counterrevolutionary after he had interrupted a royal session in the Tuileries by shouting for justice.[17]

Having been disappointed by the king, ministers, nobility, courts, committees, and now the deputies as a whole, Morizot decided to take his case to the public. The titles of his pamphlets trace a path of one failure after another. In 1790, he published first his *Denunciation against Sr. Necker, Prime Minister of Finances, and against Sr. Lambert, Controller-General, Submitted to the Reports Committee of the National Assembly*, then his *Denunciation to the National Assembly against the Bureaus of Its Reports Committee*, and finally his *Appeal to the King, in the Presence of the Nation, and Under the Eyes of Europe, of a Denial of Justice by the National Assembly, Containing a Historical Essay on the Troubles Caused in Every Empire by Lawyers, and an Abridged Discussion of the Current Revolution, Its Operations, and Its Effects.* In furious, frenzied prose, he recounted everything that had befallen him over the last two years. "Who will win this revolution?" he asked. "Those who make it and champion it, the intriguers, the liars, and the rascals," adding, in a footnote, "I might have added actors and executioners, because they are active citizens and I am not, despite my forty years of study and service, because all my revenue can be expressed by a zero. Figures derange the equality established by the decrees."[18] The French, Morizot asserted, were living "among the debris of a ruined monarchy, now converted into a bourgeois aristocracy."[19] The last of these pamphlets ended with a note from the publisher explaining that Morizot had fallen ill before it could be printed. He had been unable to correct the proofs.

What, exactly, was Morizot's problem? It is worth noting that none of the actors involved in his drama seem to have disputed the fundamental legitimacy of his complaint. It may be tempting to attribute his troubles to his belligerence, paranoia, and propensity for violence—those potential allies whom he did not put off with his insults he scared off with his death threats. And yet many people with these same qualities thrived in the French Revolution. Could it have been that Morizot's stubborn faith in the beneficence of the king alienated the deputies who were supposed to be working on his behalf? In fact, there is no clear pattern of political allegiance dividing his advocates from his adversaries. His opponent Ricard may have been a member of the Jacobin Club, but so were several of Morizot's supporters. His supporter Digoine may have been a royalist, but so it seems were many of his opponents.[20] Could there have been a conspiracy between Ricard and Necker, as Morizot suspected? The deputy and the minister are known to have corresponded regarding political matters early in the Revolution and to have dined together on at least one occasion, so the possibility cannot be entirely ruled out.[21] But it seems unlikely that Necker would have had the time, energy, or inclination to organize such a massive plot against such a minor character. He had more pressing affairs. Was the problem that the National Assembly really didn't give a damn? In fact, the evidence all points in the opposite direction. It really did. Far too many hours and pages were filled with discussion of Morizot's case.

The National Assembly gave a damn, just a strange one. If everyone agreed that Morizot deserved justice, why not simply grant it to him? Why make him produce so much paperwork? Why keep sending him down the hall to yet another clerk, yet another office? As he wrote in one of his pamphlets, he was fed up with being told by these politicians and administrators "that the problem does not belong to their department. To their department! Does truth have departments, where it can be suffocated? Can the confidence of king be divided up into departments, like any other operation? Are the oppressed of one department any less the subjects of the king than those of the departments of the Ministries of the Navy or Foreign Affairs?"[22] He could not understand that while he wondered, confused, how the king's sovereign and absolute power could ever be divided, the deputies were wondering, enthused, exactly the same thing.

It must have been hard. The comfort he had once taken in knowing that somebody was ultimately responsible for ensuring that justice be done had been taken away. He wanted to petition deputies the way he had once petitioned the king, but they could no more decide his case on their own initiative than they could cure his scrofula by touch. He wished to solicit them the way he had once solicited princesses—he complained, for instance, that Mirabeau had agreed to serve as his "patron" in Versailles, only to snub him in Paris[23]—but discreetly perfumed letters had lost their spell. What he needed was the right signature on the proper letterhead. Everyone agreed that it was an outrage that he had lost his job to the king's aunt's chambermaid's nephew. But one arbitrary use of power could not be corrected by another.

He was going to have to gather his supporting documents, take them to the right office, and wait his turn. A world of privilege was becoming a world of rights; the personal state was becoming the personnel state.

"Shareholders in the Great Social Enterprise"

Posterity is in no position to condescend. Two centuries later, we still have a hard time gathering our papers and getting them to the right place. And we still have trouble adjusting to the fact that the person on the other end of the counter or telephone line or chain of correspondence will not simply solve our problems. Even those of us most attached to liberal and democratic values—to diligence and process and everything else that is our due—occasionally succumb, like this poor clerk, to the fantasy that an omnipotent, but benevolent authority might intervene in our case, that some supervisor in some office somewhere will ultimately recognize the legitimacy of our demand and satisfy it, even if it means breaking a few rules, circumventing a few regulations. The wish behind such a fantasy is easy enough to discern: the wish for a good father, to be sure, but above all the wish to get things done and get on with our lives.

The parchments and papers of the Old Regime recorded centuries of such special arrangements, mediating between the sovereign power and the individuals, communities, and other corporate bodies that were subject to it. The need for these records was a commonplace of early modern political thought. "In the Institution or Acquisition of a Common-wealth, which is independent, there needs no Writing," Hobbes explained in *The Leviathan*, "because the Power of the Representative has there no other bounds, but such as are set out by the unwritten Law of Nature." Political society was founded by a speech act; the social contract was an oral one. Parchments and papers appeared once it became necessary to establish the specific modalities of subjection. As Hobbes wrote, "in subordinate bodies, there are such diversities of Limitation necessary, concerning their businesses, times, and places, as can neither be remembered without Letters, nor taken notice of, unlesse such Letters be Patent, that they may be read to them, and withall sealed, or testified, with the Seales, or other permanent signes of the Authority of the Soveraign."[24] French theorists of absolutism from Jean Bodin to Jacob-Nicholas Moreau echoed these arguments.

Control over all these records was no small matter. The monarchy, the parlements, and various corporate bodies routinely mobilized archival resources in their struggles over representation, taxation, and other pressing issues. A survey from 1770 estimated that there were some 5,700 document depositories across France, most of them jealously guarded by feudal, monastic, and municipal authorities wary of the state's tendency to withdraw their privileges and then offer them back at a premium.[25] The Maurist scholars Toustain and Tassin, in their monumental treatise on the science of "diplomatics," attempted a comprehensive nomenclature, filling hundreds of pages with descriptions of *accords, acommodemens, actes, anathématismes, annotations, arrêts, articles, assignations, assignats, autorités, aveux, avis, bénéfices, billets, bills, brefs, brévets, bulletins, capitulaires, cartulaires, catalogues, cédules, certifications, certificats, chartes, chirographes, citations, concordats, conscriptions, constitutions, contrats, conventions, copies, dénombremens, dispositions, échanges, écrits, écritures, édits, endentures, enquêtes, enseignemens, épitres, évidences, gesta, grosses, indicules, inscriptions, invectives, inventaires, jugemens, lettres, libelles, lièves, livres, mandats, mandemens, matricules, mémoires, minutes, montres, monumens, notices, oblations, obligations, opuscules, ordonnances, pactes, pages, papiers terriers, pragmatiques, préceptes, privilèges, procédures, procès, procès-verbaux, procurations, protestations, protocoles, quittances, réformations, registres, renonciations, réponses, rescriptions, rescrits, rôles, sanctions, sermens, status, syngraphes, tables, testamens, tomi chartarum, traités, transactions, vidimus*—and even this was only a partial list, since the authors listed, for example, more than thirty different kinds of *brefs*, from the *bref de serment* (itself comprising *breve sacrementi* and *breve sacramentum*) to the *breve pro quæsta* (described as "fort à la mode au XIII. & XIV. siècles").[26]

"Fish skins and dragon intestines," the *Encyclopédie* commented snarkily.[27] Alexis de Tocqueville remains the most subtle analyst of the Enlightenment's disenchantment with this regime. "Above the real society, whose constitution was still traditional, confused, and irregular, where law remained varied and contradictory, ranks were separated, status was fixed, and burdens were unequal," he wrote, "there was slowly built an imaginary society in which everything appeared simple and coordinated, uniform, equitable, and in accord with reason."[28] The vocabulary of imagination and appearance is important here. Like Guillauté's file wheels, the forces that Tocqueville gathered under the term "centralization" were less real than aspirational. Or if they were real, like any number of ministeral reforms undertaken in the seventeenth and eighteenth centuries, their reality tended to be partial, fleeting, and vulnerable to the vagaries of jurisdictional disputes, court intrigue, and other complications. Indeed, even the *intendants*, whom historians since Tocqueville have presented as the most "modern" of Old Regime officials, routinely found themselves forced to compromise with local rights and privileges that some villager had managed to excavate from a town archive. But the imagination was also powerful. More and more French men and women were drawn to the idea that the state could be simple and coordinated, uniform and equitable. Nor was this a matter of a few *philosophes*: There was mass support across France for a reform of the conditions under which official documents were produced, reproduced, and exchanged.[29]

Historians of political thought have tended to treat the conjuncture of 1787–89 as a crisis in modes of political representation. The hero of this narrative is Emmanuel-Joseph Sieyès, who emerged from relative obscurity as a midlevel church administrator to become the most influential polemicist, political theorist, and legislator in the nation. The pamphlets that he published between November 1788 and May 1789—the *Views on the Means of*

Execution Available to the Representatives of France in 1789, the *Essay on Privileges*, and *What Is the Third Estate?*—pointed the way to the formation of the National Assembly in June, the promulgation of the Declaration of the Rights of Man and Citizen in August, the reorganization of France's territory in December and January, and the drafting of the nation's first constitution in the months that followed.

Like Oedipus at Thebes, Sieyès discovered a timely solution to a riddle, one that threatened to consume the delegates who had gathered in Versailles for the meeting of the Estates General. The Sphinx in this case was Rousseau, and the riddle concerned the role of political representation in the life cycle of the nation. "The instant a People gives itself Representatives," Rousseau warned in *The Social Contract*, "it ceases to be free; it ceases to be."[30] The happiest societies, Rousseau maintained, were those in which all members could congregate beneath an oak tree to regulate collective affairs in person, unmediated. This was a seductive image, especially in the warmer months, but of little help to the hundreds of provincial administrators, lawyers, and businessmen who were struggling to justify their roles to themselves and the nation they were suddenly claiming to represent. France consisted of some 26 million people; not even a metaphorical tree would be able to accommodate them all at once. How could the general will express itself over such an extensive and populous territory without destroying its liberty, without endangering its very existence?

In a scene that has played itself out over and over again in histories of the French Revolution, Sieyès discovered the riddle's solution in the same political modernity that served as its pretext.[31] As societies became larger and more complex, he argued, they were forced to divide up tasks between members. Some cultivated grain, others wove cloth, still others exchanged these products. This division of labor led to greater levels of efficiency and prosperity; it was the foundation of social progress. A time would come when the labor of politics would also have to be made into a specialized task. "In bringing all the faculties of your mind to bear only on a part of the totality of useful labors, you will obtain a greater product with less effort and less expense," he wrote in one version of this argument. "This separation is to the advantage of all the members of society. It belongs to political labors just as to all genres of productive labor. The common interest, the improvement of the social state itself, cries out to us to make government a particular profession."[32] This basic argument, which Sieyès first developed in his manuscripts from the 1770s—he would later boast that he had realized the importance of the division of labor before he read Adam Smith's *The Wealth of Nations*—was elaborated and refined throughout his career. It was a fresh, modern, and ultimately revolutionary argument for representative government.

There is another element to Sieyès's solution, however, that historians have largely overlooked. Here, too, he was responding to a challenge posed in its most forceful form by Rousseau. "The books and all of the accounts of financial administrators serve less to detect their infidelities than to disguise them," Rousseau had warned in his article on political economy for the *Encyclopédie*. "So set aside the registers and papers, and put the finances back in faithful hands; that is the only way that they might be faithfully managed."[33] Similiar criticisms could be found throughout his political works; he disapproved of paperwork with the same passion that he disapproved of all forms of written communication. It was yet another one of those "dangerous supplements" that kept him up nights.[34]

With a bit of tinkering, Sieyès invented a system by which political representation and paperwork could work together to neutralize their respective dangers. We can see this invention in progress in his first political pamphlet, the *Views of the Executive Means Available to the Representatives of France in 1789*.[35] When the monarchy, overwhelmed with debt, took the drastic step of summoning the Estates General in July 1788, it also solicited advice on what form the meeting should take. Should it resemble the previous meeting of the estates, which had been in 1614? Should it resemble some earlier incarnation? This call for proposals offered anyone who could form an opinion and afford a printer an opportunity to intervene in the public sphere. Many turned to the historical record in search of useable pasts; Sieyès dismisses their efforts as a "gothic frenzy." At the same, he expresses impatience with the "good intentions" of the philosophers. "The glance of the administrator," he writes in the opening pages of the pamphlet, "searches out the means of execution."[36]

This glance looked to paperwork for solutions. Sieyès's pamphlet provided detailed instructions to the members of the Estates General on how to proceed after seizing power. One of the first orders of business would be to appoint four committees to reform the nation's finances. The first would produce a statement of current income and expenditures; the second, a projection of future expenses; the third, a model of future taxation; and the fourth, a report on the work of the first three committees. Each of these committees would be given "a special order to divide its work into as many different parts as can then be separately and fully examined and verified." Above all, "whenever it has to submit a partial report to the assembly, it will deposit all its paperwork in the registry for detailed inspection by those members who might want to examine it more closely."[37] The *word* of the committees was not enough; their work was too complicated and too important to be left to a mode of communication as ephemeral as speech.

Of course there was nothing especially innovative, let alone revolutionary, about demanding that the committees write things down. After all, this practice dates to the Bronze Age. The revolution came next, when this paperwork was made public. Not only news of the paperwork—the free-press solution favored by the U.S. Constitution, for example—but the paperwork itself. Sieyès offered the joint-stock company as a model. "The salaries of these agents and administrators, and, in general, all expenditure of the public establishment is met by annual tax revenue," he writes. "Thus citizens who pay taxes should be considered to be shareholders in the great social enterprise. They supply its capital; they are its masters."[38] Sieyès was by no means the first political theorist to propose the joint-stock company as a model for the modern state; C. B. Macpherson famously and controversially attributes the idea to Locke.[39] Unlike Locke, however, Sieyès extended this analogy to practices of public accounting. The state would have to open its books and it would have to keep them open. Only paperwork would guarantee that the social enterprise remained accountable to the citizen-shareholders. The alternative was the nightmarish scenario envisioned by Rousseau: "If the mandated agents and administrators are left to their own devices, if they were not accountable, if they were to free themselves from their dependence upon the body of shareholders, they could not but make themselves into a separate interest, an interest that would live at the expense of the general interest. They would be its masters."[40]

The Disciplined State

When Sieyès, working on his plan for a revolution in paperwork during the final months of 1788, called upon France to cast aside the "apocryphal, obscure, unintelligible" papers and parchments that formed the basis of its political culture, he could hardly have imagined what would come next. In the summer of 1789, peasants and villagers across France set fire to the parchments and papers of the Old Regime. Seigneurial records went up in flames. So, too, the archives of notaries, court clerks, tax farmers, and religious orders. In the Mâconnais, posters circulated, apparently in both manuscript and printed forms, proclaiming "By order of the king, the people of the countryside are permitted to go into all of the chateaux of the Mâconnais to ask for the feudal registers. If their requests are refused, they can sack, burn, and pillage. No harm will come to them."[41] In Normandy, the peasants who liberated the archives of a local seigneur wrote out a receipt for the documents and signed it in the name of "the Nation."[42]

The crowds that stormed the Bastille found only seven prisoners, but over four hundred cartons of documents, stashed away
in an archive that had been described, several years earlier, as
"somber, humid, and in such unsatisfactory shape that one can
hardly find the papers, even though they are indicated by registers and repertories that have been kept with the greatest preci-
sion."[43] There were documents related to the four thousand or so
prisoners who had passed through the Bastille since its archives
were established in 1659, including the *lettres de cachet* and other
documents concerning their detention, the papers seized by the
police at the time of their arrest, and the correspondence they
had received while in the prison; documents belonging to the
lieutenant-general of police, including official correspondence,
the reports filed by police inspectors and spies, papers and other
materials gathered as evidence in the process of investigations,
and paperwork pertaining to the administration of the Bastille
and other prisons; the complete archives of the dungeon of Vin-
cennes, which had been closed in 1784; family papers deposited
by officials who had worked in the Bastille over the previous century; documents related to important trials involving the crimes
of lèse-majesté, misappropriation of public funds, counterfeiting
of money and cards, poisoning, and sorcery; and, finally, documents from the royal household that were considered especially
sensitive, including an assortment of family papers, peace trea-
ties, battle plans, and "printed and manuscript works on all sorts
of subjects, with jurisprudence, legislation, tactics, medicine,
chemistry all mixed together."[44] A committee immediately took
charge of these "instruments of violence," appointing a secretary
to catalogue them and provide a receipt for any that had to be
borrowed from the victors of the Bastille. Many were published
in nine volumes of *The Bastille Unveiled*. More importantly, they
were made available in a makeshift public archive, consultable
from noon to two until the end of August 1789.[45]

The final blow to the parchments and papers of the Old
Regime came neither from the fields nor from the faubourgs, but

from the halls and offices of the National Assembly. News of the destruction of provincial estates reached Paris and Versailles in the early days of August. On the night of August 4, the new deputies put forward a series of preliminary measures to relieve the burdens of feudalism. They proceeded cautiously at first, unsure of each other's limits, until Leguen de Kérangal, a deputy from Basse-Brétagne, took the floor. The parchments and papers now smoldering throughout France, he declared, had obliged men "to spend the night whacking ponds to prevent the frogs from troubling the sleep of their voluptuous seigneurs." "Who among us, Messieurs, in this century of enlightenment, would not build an expiatory pyre for these infamous parchments, and would not carry the torch to sacrifice them on the altar of the public good?" The surviving transcripts of the night's debate report that "enthusiasm seized all souls" and that "innumerable motions, each one more important than the next, were successively proposed."[46] By the morning of August 5, personal and corporate privilege had been abolished. The most brutal feudal obligations were simply declared null and void. The rest were reviewed by a series of legislative committees, to be converted, in François Furet's words, "into good bourgeois contracts."[47] Like the documents seized from the Bastille, these, too, would be made available to citizens, deposited in the newly formed National Archives, whose first director, Armand-Gaston Camus, was appointed that same night. The National Archives would soon be open to the public on Mondays, Thursdays, and Saturdays from nine in the morning to two in the afternoon.[48]

Charles Tilly has rightly emphasized the extent to which French state formation in the revolutionary period took place through a series of "desperate improvisations."[49] But like all improvisations, they were recognizable as such only because there were structures and rhythms in place to give them meaning. Of the first deputies, nearly half had held office under the Old Regime and a quarter had worked as lawyers.[50] This meant that at least three-quarters of the new political class had previous experience handling the parchments and papers of the Old Regime. This common previous experience, however, did not mean that they had previous experience in common. The heterogeneity of the regime's conditions largely prevented that. Their cohesion, such as it was, was mediate, rather than immediate. It was construed through a limited number of political languages that they had learned to speak and write in the networks of publication, correspondence, commerce, and academic, lodge, and salon sociabilities constituting the Enlightenment public sphere.

It was in these languages that the deputies proceeded to raise and answer, sometimes hastily, sometimes hesitantly, a series of unprecedented questions: How could national sovereignty be instituted and exercised at the local level? How could political power be distributed or divided among different branches and levels of government? How could the responsibility of public officials, both elected and appointed, be ensured? How could the state best devise and execute the "combinations of money and force" that Sieyès had defined as the basic procedure of government?[51] There would need to be registers, receipts, reports, instructions, circulars, signatures, countersignatures, seals, and other forms of official communication, just as there had been under the Old Regime. But as Sieyès had demanded, this paperwork would now ensure that public agents could go about the business of government without, at least in principle, attenuating the unity and integrity of national sovereignty.

The new ethos of paperwork was embodied by Article 15 of the Declaration of the Rights of Man and Citizen: "Society has the right to ask all public agents to give an accounting of their administration." This article has been largely neglected by the secondary literature on the French declaration, despite its evident importance.[52] Its closest relative, Article 1, Section 9 of the U.S. Constitution, merely required that "a regular statement and account of receipts and expenditures of all public money shall be published from time to time." Mason proposed that even such a report be published annually, but Madison replied that this would be overly burdensome.[53] Article 15 promised something more radical and ambitious. Less than a decade after Necker caused an international sensation with his *Comte rendu au roi*, the publication of which offered the public an unprecedented peek into the carefully edited accounts of the monarchy, accountability was now recognized as an inalienable, individual right. It would become the foundation of representative government.

Article 15 was one of the last articles to be debated by the Constituent Assembly and one of the least controversial, approved exactly as drafted by the Sixth Bureau, the office responsible for producing a text for legislative debate.[54] Curiously, none of the other proposals for the Rights of Man had formulated the right to accountability quite so expansively. Even Sieyès, in his first proposal for a declaration, merely suggested that "public officials, in all the kinds of power, are responsible for their prevarications and their conduct," excluding the king, who was inviolable.[55] The version presented by the Constitution Committee, which included Sieyès, proposed two articles on this theme: "The representatives of the nation must monitor [*surveiller*] the employment of subsidies, and by consequence, the administrators of public funds must give them an exact account" and "Ministers and other agents of royal authority are responsible for all infractions that they commit against the laws, no matter what orders they received; they must be punished for these infractions through the proceedings of the representatives of the nation."[56] There was accountability in financial affairs, responsibility in all others. The ideas of accountability and responsibility were then condensed into a single article by the deputy Thouret in his proposal of August 1, 1789, with an additional innovation. Sieyès's original proposal had not specified to whom public agents were accountable. The draft presented by the Constitution Committee had made public agents accountable to the representatives of the nation. Thouret's proposal now extended this to "all citizens": "They have the right to require of all public agents or officials an account of their conduct and to hold them responsible for their prevarications."[57] Sieyès was soon advocating for similar language: "Public officials, in all kinds of power, are responsible for their prevarications and accountable for their conduct."[58]

But it was the version of the Sixth Bureau that triumphed. Antoine de Baecque suggests that Article 15 was authored by Pierre-Hubert Anson, a moderate deputy whose ideas combined "the audacity of the Enlightenment and the wise simplicity of the methodical financier."[59] The discussion over the article took place on August 26, the penultimate day of debates. The debate was brief, since the deputies were eager to move on to drafting the constitution after a difficult week. Certain deputies suggested collapsing it into the previous article on the necessity of taxation; others wanted to combine it with the subsequent article on the necessity of the division or separation of powers. In its draft for the declaration, the Sixth Bureau had followed the article on accountability with an article that read: "All societies in which the guarantee of rights is not assured and the separation of powers not determined do not have a true Constitution."[60] Intervening in the debates, the deputy Alexandre de Lameth proposed combining the article on accountability with this article to produce a single article: "No people can enjoy liberty if the public powers are not distinct and separated and if the agents of the executive power are not responsible for their administration." For Lameth, liberty depended on holding the executive responsible to the legislative power. The deputy Duport then suggested a revision with only an implicit reference to the separation of powers: "All agents of the executive power are responsible for their administration, and the nation has the right to require an accounting." This proposal effectively brought together accountability, responsibility, and the nation while limiting accountability and responsibility to the agents of the executive power. Another deputy spoke up to suggest that the word "nation" in Duport's proposal be replaced by the word "society," because "every member of society has the right to require the responsibility of the administrator." These

43

two ideas were brought back together by Reubell, referring this time to the division of powers, rather than to their separation: "The rights of man in society are not assured unless powers are divided and public agents responsible for their administration." Finally, a deputy interrupted to remind his colleagues that the constitution still had to be written. The Sixth Bureau's version of the article on accountability was adopted unanimously. The principle of the separation of powers was placed in Article 16.[61]

The choice of the word "accountability" over the word "responsibility" was a choice for paperwork, since the former term, unlike the latter, carried with it the connotation of records, accounts, registers, and receipts. Every action or transaction undertaken by any person with or on behalf of the state had to be documented in certain anticipation of an eventual accounting. The choice of the word "society" over the words "nation" and "representatives" was equally significant. The right to call into account belonged neither to the nation, as an abstract entity, nor only to the representatives who scrutinized on its behalf. Society, every member of society, had the right to keep track of the state and thus to ensure that his interests were being accurately and effectively represented. Sieyès's plan had been executed: paperwork had become a technology of political representation.

A Stranger to Everything Happening

What about poor Morizot? Even if he had been more personable, even if his opponents had been less powerful, even if the committee members had been more capable, even if he had seen things more clearly, his dossier would still have had to share attention with the 19,356 others submitted to the Reports Committee during the first two years of the Revolution. Each of these dossiers was received by a clerk named Garnier, who recorded it in a register and filed it alphabetically in a carton before signaling its arrival to a clerk named Vaillaint, who, when not busy keeping the minutes of the committee meetings, removed the dossier from its carton and recorded in a master register the date of its arrival, the name of its reporter, the date it was assigned to that reporter, the dates of all correspondence related to it, the date that the reporter issued his report, and the decision of the committee. Clerks named Chaulay and Chachoin made copies of all letters and other documents before they were sent to ministries, tribunals, departments, districts, municipalities, National Guard posts, or private citizens; they also made summaries of all these documents in order to facilitate the study and deliberation of the committee members. Two more clerks, Hussent and Dupuis, took care of the mailing itself and, when that was done, assisted the other clerks.[62]

In its first two years of existence, the Reports Committee composed 13,842 letters. This is an impressive number until one multiplies the twenty thousand dossiers opened during that period by the number of letters required for a single case such as Morizot's.[63] Indeed, Morizot was far from the only citizen facing a delay. By the time the Constituent Assembly dissolved at the end of September 1791, the committee had accumulated 237 cartons of documents, 70 of which consisted of dossiers still open, investigations still ongoing, complaints still unresolved, citizens still desperate.[64] As the committee's president noted in an August 1791 account of its activities, "the most important affairs and a large portion of the others have been dealt with, but, despite the activity of the members who compose the committee, many affairs remain, and they will still require a lot of time." Citizens like Morizot were uncertain of where to address themselves when they had a problem, so they wrote their local or national representatives. These officials were often equally uncertain of how to proceed, and thus tended to pass the paperwork along. This was only to be expected under current conditions, the committee president explained. "As long as the constitution is not entirely finished and well understood, the different powers that it establishes are not at the height of their activity and the lines established to demarcate between them are not felt by all citizens, the French people's confidence in the National Assembly will attract to it a mass of petitions of all genres, both from the administrative corps and individuals."[65] He expressed confidence that citizens, administrators, and legislators alike would eventually grow accustomed to the new conditions.

Meanwhile, the *Royal Almanach* for 1791 offered citizens detailed instructions on how to navigate the committees of the National Assembly. The Pensions Committee received by far the most attention. All over France, there were men like Morizot who had worked for the king for decades in anticipation of a comfortable retirement. The deputies were determined to ensure that they were properly cared for. After explaining the committee's structure, the *Almanach* advised its readers that

> the necessity of avoiding all pretext of preference, the desire to bring the man living alone and retired in the provinces within range so that he can be heard as easily and promptly as those who live or have relations in the heart of the capital, have caused the committee to suspend, until October 1, the examination of the memoirs that have been or will be brought to it. The examination will then start with the oldest people first. They ordinarily have less time to enjoy and more needs to satisfy.[66]

In the meantime, citizens who believed that they were owed money by the state were invited to send their requests to the committee, where they would be duly registered by its clerks.

> If those who bring their memoirs desire them to be registered in their presence, they can demand it after waiting their turn according to the order in which they arrived.—If, independently of the presentation of a memoir, one believes it indispensable to talk to the members of the committee, one can present oneself at the day and time indicated. But this will be useless with certain members, in particular: they have ceased to receive visitors in person, to say anything themselves.[67]

It was better to put one's request on paper, with name, address, age, services provided to the state, salary, and any other compensation received, all indicated exactly. "One will find at the secretariat of the committee sheets drawn up according to the plan, in which one has only to fill in what is particular to one's case. Pensioners can join any supporting documents that they want to provide." Or almost any. An additional note suggested the egalitarian ambitions of the new ethos of paperwork: "All memoirs will be seen and examined. It thus suffices to expose the facts in a clear and precise manner. Letters of recommendation will be perfectly useless; they might even become dangerous, in that they can foster the belief that one is soliciting as a favor or a grace what one does not have the right to obtain through justice."[68] This depersonalization of power, the source of so many complaints in the years, decades, and centuries ahead, was a revolutionary accomplishment.

Did Edme-Etienne Morizot contact the Pensions Committtee? If so, he did not mention it alongside his other efforts to find his way in the new regime. Morizot published several more pamphlets over the course of 1791 and 1792. There was the *Plea to the Queen, Invoking the Attention of the August Houses of Bourbon and Austria, on the Justice Emanating from the Throne*, which probably dates from 1791; the *Abridged Tableau of the Espiegleries of the Court during the First Six Months of 1792, Serving as a Continuation of the Eleven Preceding Memoirs*; and the *Placet to Citizen Rolland, Minister of the Interior, against Citizen Boullanger, Juge de Paix of the Garde-Françaises Section, formerly L'Oratoire*, published in 1792. It is impossible to reconstruct his trajectory on the basis of these pamphlets, which are even less coherent than the first three. The archives are not much help, either. But it is clear that his situation did not improve with time. The pamphlets tend toward the wildly counterrevolutionary, with invocations of Burke and Bossuet and appeals to the émigrés, but they are also full of bitterness toward the king, who had failed to come to his rescue. "I still have a king," Morizot wrote, "but he seems to have neither ears nor guts."[69] The tribunals continued to declare themselves unfit to decide his case: "If my cause had been susceptible to an unfavorable judgment, it would have found easy access to the tribunals, and I would not have lacked judges to condemn me."[70] An unfortunate encounter with Boullanger, justice of the peace, led to twenty-six days in prison: "What an existence! Is it republican or monarchical? What measure must I take to vegetate in peace?"[71] Morizot explained to his readers that "I live isolated, withdrawn from all society, frequenting only a few victims like myself, who do not feed on public papers, who never run after the news, and who are strangers to everything that is happening."[72]

This last claim was not quite true. He was in contact about his affair with Armand de Laporte, the ultraroyalist *intendant* of the civil list. The correspondence was confiscated and published by the Legislative Assembly in 1792. He was also in contact with the other end of the political spectrum. Two of his letters were published by Jean-Paul Marat in *L'Ami du Peuple*. The first appeared in the issue of October 8, 1792. Morizot asked Marat "to announce to the public and to all of Europe that I am calling for witnesses against the rascals who administer the lotteries." His case was at last going to be heard. Danton had asked Clavière, the minister of finance, "to finally give me the justice that I have been soliciting in vain for sixteen years, while reduced to living without bread, without linens, without furniture or a home, and on charity." After his years of suffering, justice was going to be done: "It is good that these administrators, who have been fooling the public for such a long time, are finally being unmasked and the ministry forced to render a stunning justice. Let these perverts know that their intrigues did not succeed in having me massacred." This victory belonged, above all, to the French people, "whom I have always loved and defended, often at the peril of my liberty and my life, and always at my own expense."[73]

Morizot concluded with a plea to any administrators with knowledge of his affair: "I hope to finally have their archives communicated to me, if they have not burned them. I invite the former commissioner Dorival, if he is an honest man, to reveal what he knows, for the sake of the public interest, and I invite colporteurs, wandering clerks, receivers, and clerks who have been let go, in both Paris and the departments, to furnish me with their information."[74] Morizot's second letter to Marat was published on July 14, 1793. Sent from Baume-les-Dames, in the Department of the Doubs, near the Swiss border, it called for a change in the way military officers were provisioned while en route to their destinations in order to prevent financial abuses by suppliers. This letter from Morizot, entirely inconsequential, was the very last item in the very last issue of *L'Ami du Peuple*.

CHAPTER TWO

The Demon of Writing

In 1802, the journalists Charles-Guillaume Étienne and Alphonse Martainville published a history of the French theater from the beginning of the Revolution. One of its footnotes told a strange story, reproducing a letter from Collot d'Herbois, of the Committee of Public Safety, to Fouquier-Tinville, of the Revolutionary Tribunal, ordering the prosecutor to sentence the actors and actresses of the Comédie-Française on July 1, 1794. Anticipating the verdict, crowds gathered along the streets to watch these celebrities escorted to the guillotine. But the celebrities never showed up. The trial had been postponed because the paperwork had gone missing. It had been stolen, Étienne and Martainville wrote, by "a simple employee of the Committee of Public Safety named Charles-Hippolyte Labussière, who, risking his life, removed all the documents that were supposed to form the act of accusation." Not only had he removed these official documents, he had then destroyed them "in the most ingenious way." The clerk "went to the baths, soaked all of the documents until they were almost reduced to paste, and then launched them, in small pellets, through the window of the bathing room into the river." The Terror came to an end before new papers could be drawn up. The footnote concluded by claiming that the members of the Comédie-Française had not been the only ones rescued by Labussière: "More than two hundred people owe him their existence."[1]

Interest was piqued. A skeptical reader sought out Labussière in person to confirm the footnote's claims and left the meeting

convinced that the clerk had in fact rescued even more people than
the two hundred or so already attributed to him. The reader sent
a long letter to the quasi-official *Journal des Débats* in June 1802
sharing the dramatic details of how Labussière, as an employee
in the Committee of Public Safety's Prisoners Bureau, had managed to soak and shred the files of prisoners before they reached
the Revolutionary Tribunal. The letter called on all of France to
celebrate "the humanity of a simple individual to whom we owe
the preservation of more than twelve hundred victims condemned
to perish for their virtues, their wealth, or their talents."[2]

And so France did. In 1802, Labussière's portrait, since lost,
appeared in the Salon. In 1803, the Comédie-Française staged
a benefit performance of *Hamlet*—the first in France in nearly
twenty years—to an audience that included Napoleon and Josephine Bonaparte, who seem to have believed that she, too, was
one of those saved by the clerk.[3] In 1804, the authorized biography, *Charles, ou Mémoires historiques de M. de la Bussière, ex-employé
au Comité de Salut Public*, hit the shelves of French booksellers
with a long list of Terror survivors who had its protagonist to
thank. And over the next two centuries, the story would be nov-
elized, dramatized, serialized, filmed, even made for television.
Politicians, historians, and critics would debate its meaning and
merits. A bronze plaque in Labussière's honor is affixed to the
wall of the Comédie-Française; a seafood dish in his honor is a
fixture of French cuisine.

The Terror and its traumas have been credited with everything from the rise of new dance fads to the emergence of modern
liberalism.[4] It would certainly be possible to read this story and
its reception as another example of the collective effort by the
French to work through the terrible things that they had done
to one another in their desperate efforts to secure the nation
from its enemies. The postrevolutionary celebrations of Labussière's heroics seem to provide, to borrow a phrase from the film
critic J. Hoberman, "feel-good entertainment about the ultimate
feel-bad experience."[5] This chapter, however, will pursue a more

Figure 4. Labussière (portrayed by Jean d'Yd) and a collaborator (Nicholas Koline) destroying documents in Abel Gance's *Napoléon* (1927).

materialist line of interpretation. Labussière's story, I will argue, tells us less about individual agency than about the conditions under which it can emerge, its reception less about how the French relived or relieved past traumas than about how they invented new myths to resolve the contradictions in those conditions. This is a story about the materiality of communication; a story, in a word, about paperwork.[6]

Between the summers of 1793 and 1794, Year II of the Republic, the year of the Terror, the Committee of Public Safety deployed incalculable numbers of pens and papers in the name of national security. And time and again, its forces failed it. The medium that made state power possible also sporadically, spontaneously, rendered it impossible. In the months and years following the Terror, participants would come forward with harrowing tales of its paperwork. Former committee members would recount how it had overwhelmed their physical and moral faculties. Former clerks would relate how it had enabled daring acts of subterfuge and sabotage. One of these clerks, Labussière, would become a lasting symbol of paperwork and its contradictions.

"The Demon of Writing"

On October 10, 1793, Saint-Just took the floor of the National Convention to request emergency powers for its Committee of Public Safety. "Your wisdom and the just wrath of patriots have not yet vanquished the evil that everywhere contends with the people and the Revolution," he told his fellow deputies. The Republic faced war in Europe, rebellion in the provinces, tumult in the capital, and shortages of raw and cooked materials nearly everywhere. Finally, there was too much paperwork. "I have no idea how Rome and Egypt governed without this resource; they thought a great deal, and wrote little," he said. "The prolixity of the government's correspondence and orders is a sign of its inertia; it is impossible to govern without brevity." With a metaphorical flourish, he conjured up a "demon of writing" to account for these troubles: "The demon of writing is waging war against

54

Figure 5. Saint-Just (portrayed by Abel Gance) inspecting the Committee of Public Safety's archives in Abel Gance's *Napoléon* (1927).

us; we are unable to govern." When he was done, the deputies, whether persuaded, intimidated, or both, agreed to his demands, suspending the new constitution and declaring the government "revolutionary until the peace."[7] The dictatorship was in place.

Saint-Just may well have had Rousseau in mind as he composed his speech. As we saw in the last chapter, the philosopher had stressed paperwork's dangers. "The books and all of the accounts of financial administrators serve less to detect their infidelities than to disguise them," Rousseau had written in his article on political economy for the *Encyclopédie*. "So set aside the registers and papers, and put the finances back in faithful hands; this is the only way that they might be faithfully managed."[8] Elsewhere, he heaped contempt on "the terrifying multitudes of edicts and declarations that one sees emanating daily from some courts," which showed the people that "even the sovereign does not know what he wants."[9] The writing practices that were meant to extend the power of the sovereign across space and time simultaneously threatened sovereignty's unity and integrity. Such concerns reflected Rousseau's critique of writing as a threat to sincerity, authenticity, self-presence, and other virtues, a critique that resonated throughout revolutionary political culture, particularly the Jacobin subculture from which Saint-Just had emerged.

But the war against the demon of writing was about more than metaphysics. Since the summer of 1789, the deputies had indeed tried entrusting not just finances, but all administration to more faithful and capable hands. The Declaration of the Rights of Man and Citizen had promised that officials would be elected or selected on the basis of their merits and talents alone. But while the Revolution had made real progress against venality, for example, it remained almost entirely helpless against a far more mundane and pervasive form of corruption, the corruption of its texts. Saint-Just's demonic metaphor was not at all a bad one for the material and semiotic mishaps that sporadically spoiled the manuscripts of even the most meritorious, talented public servants.

Meanwhile, so much had come to depend on paperwork's success. "Each hour that you consecrate to this work, each line that you inscribe in the register, is a step forward for the Revolution; each obstacle that you alleviate is a victory against the enemies of the country," the philosopher-legislator Condorcet exhorted local administrators in February 1792. "Let these painstaking and tiresome functions take on a grander character in your eyes; let them be ennobled by the idea that circumstances have attached to them the fate of French liberty and perhaps that of the human species."[10] Thousands and thousands of men—nobody knew exactly how many or how to contact them all—were struggling to complete their paperwork promptly and accurately, a daunting task, even under the best of circumstances.[11] What would happen as circumstances worsened? As war raged, sedition spread, and hunger gnawed? National security was deferred and destabilized by the letters, notices, reports, tables, and registers upon which it depended.

From its inception, the Committee of Public Safety was as
concerned with paperwork as it was with public safety per se.
Its first responsibility, when the National Convention voted it
into existence in April 1793, was to ensure "the surveillance
and acceleration" of the administration.[12] The deputies hoped
that paperwork's intractable materiality, its painstaking and tiresome functionality, could be surmounted through sufficiently
rigorous measures of time and work discipline. But the mandate
contained a crucial contradiction. Surveillance and acceleration
were compatible in principle, but incompatible in practice. Every
additional report or receipt required by the committee from
national or local administrators necessarily prevented them from
the rapid performance of their other duties. Thus, the more the
committee tried to exercise its powers of surveillance, the more
it risked delays in the administration, and the more it tried to
accelerate the administration, the more it risked wavering in its
surveillance. This contradiction would organize and disorganize
the revolutionary government throughout the year of the Terror.

An order from July 1793 reads: "The Committee of Public
Safety notifies citizens that given the multitude of affairs with
which it is overburdened, it is now only able to accept requests in
writing."[13] The number of clerks assisting the committee with its
writing increased from about forty the first summer to more than
four hundred the following one; the demand for labor was so great
that many employees were hired without presenting their *certificats
de civisme*, the attestations of republican virtue required for government service.[14] The law of 14 Frimaire (December 4), which
institutionalized the dictatorship in the aftermath of Saint-Just's
attack on the demon of writing, only exacerbated the contradiction
between surveillance and acceleration. On the one hand, the law
contained a series of measures aimed at speeding the rhythms of
the state. It set detailed deadlines, for example, for proofing, printing, dispatching, and publicizing a new daily legal bulletin; delays
were punishable by five years in irons. On the other hand, the
law implemented a comprehensive new program of administrative

surveillance that required authorities across the nation to set aside whatever they were doing in order to report back to Paris every ten days—the *décade* of the revolutionary calendar—with a full account of their activities. New national agents were appointed to monitor compliance; they, too, were to report back every ten days. In the law's most extraordinary measure, conversation between officials was now prohibited: "All relations between all public functionaries can no longer take place except in writing."[15] It was an implausible, even impossible demand, but it reflected the committee's need—both real and imagined—for the kinds of knowledge and power that could be worked out only on paper.

Some sense of how this paperwork was supposed to work is conveyed by a flow chart for the Bureau for the Surveillance of the Execution of the Laws, which was opened in late 1793 to process the reports arriving every ten days from throughout France.[16] At the top of the chart was "General Surveillance," which was divided between the "external surveillance of all public functions" and the "internal surveillance of the operations of the bureau." External surveillance took place through "investigations," "correspondence," and "expedition." Investigations relied on the "examination of the laws and decrees of the committee," "tables of the same organized by subject," "review of analyses of responses and accounts of ministers," "tables of the backlog of laws and decrees predating 14 Frimaire," "examination of claims of the failure to execute laws and decrees," and finally, "verification and comparison of all ten-day reports in one group, organized by subject." Correspondence involved "letters concerning measures to take and accounts to make," "drawing up circulars," "making copies of letters and circulars for signature," and "sending documents to be signed and returning those that have been signed." And the last operation of external surveillance, expedition, involved maintaining "a journal of the operations of public functionaries," "records of active and passive execution," and "the table of these two registers." The operations of internal surveillance were still more intricate. After listing the various titles of clerks within the offices of the Committee of Public Safety who assisted in the task of surveillance of execution—*rechercheurs, vérifacteurs, releveurs des lois, releveurs d'arrêtés, correspondants, copistes, expéditionnaires*—the chart proceeded to classify the documents these clerks handled, from "the original copies of letters of ministers, the executive council, and administrators organized by constituted authority" to "notices of the reception of laws," themselves divided by "communes, cantons, and districts" and then subdivided by "square division of France into east, south, north, and west." It was a system of remarkable sophistication. What new forms would the demon of writing take?

"The Physical Impossibility of Doing Otherwise"

On July 26, 1794, Robespierre threatened another purge of the National Convention. On July 27, better known by the revolutionary date of 9 Thermidor, the deputies deposed him, deposed Saint-Just, deposed Couthon. On July 28, this "triumvirate" was sent to the guillotine. And on July 29, the arduous process of political, juridical, and cultural reckoning began, exposing the nation to shocking details about the worst excesses and darkest recesses of the national-security state. The Convention formed commissions, organized tribunals, scrutinized records, summoned witnesses, and issued reports on some of the most notorious episodes and institutions of the Terror. Fouquier-Tinville, the lead prosecutor of the Revolutionary Tribunal in Paris, was tried, convicted, and sentenced to death by the court he had once controlled. So too was Carrier, the "noyeur de Nantes," who had drowned some four thousand "counterrevolutionaries" in the Loire, after a trial that lasted two months and involved more than two hundred witnesses.[17] In December 1794 came the turn of three of the surviving members of the Committee of Public Safety: Barère, Billaud-Varenne, and Collot d'Herbois. A legislative commission was established under the direction of the deputy Jean-Baptiste-Michel Saladin, himself a former political prisoner, to compile evidence and formulate charges. After two months of research and debate, the commission recommended that the Convention charge the three with "tyrannizing the French people" and "oppressing their representatives."[18] The commission's report included seventy-five appendices reproducing a small sample of what it had uncovered in the archives: arrest warrants, rendition orders, prisoner lists, interrogation transcripts. One document after another concluded with the signatures of the accused.

Of the many crimes detailed in Saladin's report, one struck contemporary observers as especially sinister. This was the formation of a Bureau for Administrative Surveillance and General Police, better known simply as the General Police Bureau. Established in April 1794 to strengthen the surveillance of government agents—the Bureau for the Surveillance of the Execution of Laws had proven too passive—the office soon exceeded its formal mandate and became a shadow security service directed by Saint-Just, Robespierre, and Couthon personally, allowing them to circumvent the already weakened protections of revolutionary justice.[19] In the right-hand column of the bureau's registers, clerks summarized incoming reports and accusations: "The commune of Faucon sends its list of former nobles as required by the decrees of 27 and 28 Germinal; there is only one, named Paul Henry de Mouret de Reviglias, chevalier of Barroux." In the left-hand column, Saint-Just, Robespierre, or, more rarely, Couthon scrawled a response: "Transfer this ex-noble to Paris." Any difficulties implementing these orders were also recorded: "It was not possible to find the department where Faucon is located."[20] Arrest warrants were prepared by a member of the Committee of Public Safety; by Augustin Lejeune, the bureau chief, whom we will encounter again shortly; or by one of the clerks working under Lejeune's supervision. In theory, though not always in practice, a minimum of three signatures—a primary signature and two cosignatures—was required for the warrant to become legal. By cosigning the bureau's warrants, the commission alleged, Barère, Billaud-Varenne, and Collot d'Herbois had colluded in its crimes.

Then, as now, pursuit of high elected officials for crimes

committed while in office required a certain degree of procedural improvisation. Rather than entrusting the case to the tribunals, the National Convention resolved to try the accused within its own halls, opening debate on March 22, 1795. The first witnesses to speak were two former colleagues from the Committee of Public Safety, the deputies Lindet and Carnot. Lindet had been in charge of provisions and subsistence during the Terror; Carnot had masterminded the war effort. They had been exempted from formal charges, but were nevertheless worried that evidence would emerge implicating them, too, in the activities of the General Police Bureau. In fact, their cosignatures appeared on multiple arrest warrants next to those of Barère, Billaud-Varenne, and Collot d'Herbois. By testifying for the accused, they were testifying for themselves. They were also attesting to their experiences managing the mass production, reproduction, and exchange of official documents in wartime.

Lindet's testimony on the first day of the trial lasted six hours. He hardly mentioned his colleagues on the Committee of Public Safety at all. Instead, he provided a detailed account of his own activities during the year of the Terror. These had been the activities of a conscientious functionary, he insisted, not a reckless ideologue. The year had been spent "continuously enclosed in the committee, aware only of what I read in the reports sent to us by the minister of the interior, the departments, and the municipalities."[21] Even his mission to Caen to put down the federalist revolt there had consisted mainly of completing "decrees, proclamations, instructions, letters, memoirs, projects, correspondence.... I did not eat at anyone's home, I did not go to any parties, to any plays; I was only the representative of the people, at every moment, day and night."[22] He avoided any direct reference to the General Police Bureau, making only one allusion to it, at the very end of the day's testimony. "No doubt," he told the deputies, his voice by now barely audible, "they will search through the twenty thousand signatures that I gave to find some text to serve as the basis for an act of accusation against me."[23]

But given so many decrees, proclamations, instructions, and other paperwork, how could one or two signatures be held against him? Lindet's strategy, in effect, was to subsume each of his signatures in the context of his twenty thousand signatures, to subsume his twenty thousand signatures in the context of the twelve times twenty thousand signatures of the Committee of Public Safety as a whole, and to subsume those twelve times twenty thousand signatures in the context of a brand new Republic struggling to make its way in a hostile world. He seems to have hoped that the inflation of signatures would lead to a reduction of their value, that is, to a diminution of the personal responsibility that such signatures were supposed to signify.

A lawyer by training, Lindet seemed to hope that he could win sympathy by presenting himself as a devoted legislator who had done his best under impossible circumstances. Carnot, by contrast, was a mathematician, engineer, and military strategist; his testimony reflected his more calculating sensibility. "People of ill will try in vain to cite some signatures made by me on acts that they find reprehensible," he said when it was his turn to speak. "It must be explained once and for all to the National Convention what a signature in the Committee of Public Safety was. This explication is necessary not only to prevent the accusations that might be directed against members of this committee who are not among the indicted, but also because it weakens the charges made against those who are, by delimiting the boundaries of the personal responsibility of each one of them." According to Carnot, signatures—or to be more precise, cosignatures, the kind most often cited by the commission as evidence—were simple formalities. A cosignature indicated only that the document in question had been seen by another member of the committee, as required by law. It was "a purely mechanical operation that proves nothing, that attests to nothing, except that the reporter, that is to say, the primary signer of the draft decree [*minute*], had acquitted himself of the prescribed formality of submitting the document in question for the examination of the committee."[24] It was a brilliant attempt at redescription. The presence of a cosignature on an illegal act did not mean that the cosigner had done something illegal; it meant that all the signers had done something legal.

Carnot even contended that the commission's report presented a variety of documents bearing his signature that he never had read and that he would never have signed had he read them. "You might ask," he said, "why, in the former Committee of Public Safety, we signed in this way documents with which we were not familiar. I respond: By absolute necessity, by the physical impossibility of doing otherwise." Here he returned to the defense set out by Lindet. He and his colleagues were simply overwhelmed by the volume of work. "The number of matters ordinarily reached four or five hundred a day. Each one of us handled, or had handled by the bureaus, those matters that belonged to his domain, and normally brought them to be signed by the others toward two or three o'clock in the morning." Under this de facto division of labor, he was no more responsible for his colleagues' offices than they were for his. Absorbed as he was in his own work, how could he ever have "guessed that it pleased Robespierre and Saint-Just to plot against the rest of us in their General Police Bureau?"[25]

Saladin was incredulous, and rightly so. Lindet and Carnot's explanations elided their real responsibility not only for the activities of the Bureau for Administrative Surveillance and General Police, but for terrorist measures more generally. While there was a significant division of labor within the committee's offices, it was never as strict as the members asserted. The surviving drafts of the General Police Bureau's decrees prove their involvement—some are even in Carnot's handwriting.[26] But the accused, following Lindet and Carnot's lead, vigorously defended themselves with seemingly commonsensical descriptions of their paperwork. "It has been observed with a sort of affectation that the signatures of the accused can be found on almost all of those acts provoked by Robespierre," Collot d'Herbois told the Convention. "The reason for this is simple: it is because we were more assiduous than the others; we were always at the committee, and so we could always be found to sign documents."[27] Barère and Billaud-Varenne argued along similar lines. There was too much paperwork; they were forced to divide their labor; their signatures were insignificant; they were not responsible. Were the deputies convinced? They never reached a final verdict. On April 1, 1795, following another uprising in the capital, the Convention declared a new state of emergency, deploying the military to maintain law and order. Barère, Billaud-Varenne, and Collot d'Herbois were ordered into exile without further debate. Lindet and Carnot went on to become ministers.

"Tiresome Details," "Barbarous Concision"

The registers indicate that the Bureau for Administrative Surveillance and General Police processed approximately four thousand reports between April and July 1794.[28] One of these reports involved an inhabitant of the Department of the Aisne, a wealthy former nobleman named Lauraguais. As a man of the Enlightenment, Lauraguais had first welcomed the Revolution, then grew uneasy with its progress. In an act of extreme audacity, if not stupidity, he had filed a complaint against local villagers for uprooting a tree on his property without permission. The villagers had selected it as their Liberty Tree. Citing Lauraguais's lack of patriotism, the General Police Bureau issued a warrant for his arrest on July 16, 1794. Lauraguais was taken into custody, transported to Paris under military escort, and imprisoned in the Conciergerie to await judgment by the Revolutionary Tribunal. Fortunately, the Terror came to an end before he could be tried. He was still angry about his experience, though, and in the months after Thermidor he published two pamphlets denouncing those responsible for his persecution. One of those singled out was Augustin Lejeune, chief of the General Police Bureau.[29]

Lejeune could not have been happy to be reading his name in print. He and Saint-Just had first met in 1791, striking up a conversation one evening at an inn outside Lâon, capital of the Aisne. At the time, Saint-Just was a local poet, playwright, and

pamphleteer; Lejeune was a clerk in the departmental administration with similarly literary ambitions. The following year, as
Saint-Just entered politics as deputy from the department to the
National Convention, Lejeune joined the army, rising to the rank
of sergeant. Wounded at Neerwinden, he moved to Paris to take a
job in the offices of the Ministry of Foreign Affairs. He had been
working there for six months when his friend, now one of the most
powerful men in France, asked him to take over the Committee of
Public Safety's new office. It was April 1794, the height of the Terror. Lejeune was just twenty-three years old.[30] One year later, with
Saint-Just dead and reviled, he found himself publicly exposed as
the supervisor of this terrifying instrument of political violence.
Although he was not legally responsible for his work as bureau
chief, there were always other, less formal kinds of retribution to
fear as the Terror turned from Red to White.

Lejeune came to his own defense in a memoir addressed to his
fellow citizens in the Aisne. He contended that he had ignored
the first two summonses to come work for the General Police
Bureau. Saint-Just had finally come in person to the offices of
the Ministry of Foreign Affairs to demand his services. No longer able to refuse, Lejeune packed his desk and moved to the
Committee of Public Safety to take control of the new bureau.
According to the memoir, Saint-Just's instructions were simple.
Every report had to conclude with one of three words: "moderate," "aristocrat," or "counterrevolutionary." The clerks' apprais-
als would serve as the basis for the deputies' decrees. One of
Lejeune's subalterns protested that these orders went against the
rule of law. The clerks could describe the individuals involved,
weigh the evidence included in the dossiers, develop the case for
and against. But they could not be judges or jurors: "How can you
invest us with the power of life and death by asking us to apply the
words that will determine your judgment? This task is beyond our
abilities! We can only analyze documents and provide you with
reports."[31] Saint-Just promptly ejected the man from the offices.
The clerks had their orders, and they were to follow them exactly.

Lejeune, however, had other plans. Once Saint-Just had safely departed, he instructed his clerks "to maintain the most exact fidelity in their reports, but also to enter into the most minor details that might exculpate and save the citizens whose destiny was in their hands." He was not so naive as to believe that these minor details would convince the committee of anyone's innocence. His hope, rather, was that by overproducing details, the bureau would underproduce reports and thus slow down the procedures of revolutionary justice. Thus, his clerks "presented five innocents for every six people denounced, and with that, tiresome details, infinite justifications." Saint-Just and Robespierre kept demanding lists of victims. Instead, they received reports, thorough reports, with all the relevant details and a few irrelevant ones as well. By Lejeune's accounting, twenty thousand denunciations arrived at the bureau: "That would have been twenty thousand citizens, some sent to the prisons, others to the scaffold, if in accordance with the wishes of Saint-Just and Robespierre we had given our operations a barbarous concision."[32] But he maintained that only 500 reports were analyzed by the General Police Bureau during this period. Of these, only 250 resulted in arrests. And of these, only 130 were brought to Paris to be judged by the Revolutionary Tribunal. This included Lauraguais.

What could be done to help these prisoners? Procedure dictated that Lejeune pass the relevant papers to the Revolutionary Tribunal for prosecution. "I sent nothing," he explains. "I allowed it to remain unaware that they were destined for it; the tribunal received neither notification, nor copies of the rendition orders, nor documents to serve as the basis for judgment, and so all of them escaped its ferocious teeth."[33] Addressing himself to Lauraguais directly, he swore that "Your existence is my proof." Saint-Just had wanted the nobleman's blood, but "a human being was there to prevent you from appearing before this tribunal of death. This human being is me."[34] Lejeune proceeded to reproduce a list of other notables from the area who had been singled out by local sans-culotte militants as "good for the guillotine."

Robespierre had told him to draw up acts of accusation against everyone whose name appeared there. "I shuddered reading this list. I brought it home with me, I lifted up a paving stone, and buried it, determined to perish rather that allow it to reach its destination."[35] Nor was this the only time his personal intervention had saved citizens from certain death. Paperwork could take lives, but it could also save them.

Lejeune's claims are unreliable, at best. He inflated the number of incoming reports fivefold; he reduced the number of outgoing decrees by half.[36] Nevertheless, even as the former bureau chief tried to minimize his culpability, he attested to the conditions and contradictions inside the Committee of Public Safety. The clerks were caught between the imperatives of surveillance, with its "tiresome details," and acceleration, with its "barbarous concision." The General Police Bureau had been the final, failed attempt to sublate this contradiction, investing the powers of surveillance and acceleration in Robespierre, Saint-Just, and Couthon personally. But paperwork had continued to defer and displace the object of power. Did Lejeune intentionally slow down the pace of political violence by burying it under paperwork? Did he then halt the violence altogether by burying the paperwork itself? No, but he could have. He seems to have recognized, if only belatedly, that the proliferation of documents and details presented opportunities for resistance, as well as for compliance. To his credit, he ceased making his claims, at least in print, once he was out of danger. He returned to work, rising to the highest ranks of the Empire's and then the Restoration's tax administration. A friend of the popular dramatist Eugène Scribe, he would devote his spare time to writing novels, the last of which was a fictional attack on the Republic and its regicides. His description of his months inside the Committee of Public Safety would apparently not be published until the 1890s, when it appeared as a "revolutionary curiosity" in an antiquarian journal. It would be left to another clerk, with a story at once more simple and more bizarre, to capture the public's imagination.

"As Simple as It Was Bizarre"

The 1802 letter to the *Journal des Débats* from the anonymous correspondent who had met Charles-Hippolyte Labussière in person would provide the basis for all subsequent versions of his story. Labussière, the letter explained, had been hired as a clerk in the Committee of Public Safety's Prisoners Bureau two months before the Thermidor coup. Each day, at two o'clock in the afternoon, he handed over documents to an agent of the Popular Commission, which had been formed earlier that year to hasten the work of the Revolutionary Tribunal. The agent neither inventoried nor provided a receipt for the twenty to twenty-five files that he was supposed to receive from the clerk at the appointed hour. His haste made possible Labussière's embezzlement. Nobody would notice if a file or two had been subtracted from the delivery, and if later it was discovered, nobody would be able to tell how, when, or where the files had gone missing. The imperatives of acceleration had subverted the rigors of surveillance.

Labussière began by hiding the documents in his desk. After the first week or so, however, this proved too dangerous. So he settled on the scheme that would make him famous. Late at night, around one o'clock, while the committee members were deliberating in another room, the clerk "would climb up to his office, go to his hiding place, take the documents, soak them in a bucket of water, and make six or seven balls out of the paste, which he would put in his pockets." Toward six o'clock in the morning, he would leave the offices for the public baths, "where he would soak these same balls of paper some more." Labussière would finally "subdivide them into smaller balls, which he would then toss into the Seine through the window of his bath." Thus soaked, shredded, and flushed, they vanished forever. The letter built toward the night of June 27, when Labussière discovered the files of the members of the Comédie-Française. Narrowly evading detection, first in the offices, then on the street, he destroyed them, too, saving the French theater. After the coup of Thermidor, he took a position as an assistant to Legendre, a sympathetic member of the Committee of General Security. In this capacity, he helped liberate still more political prisoners. He then returned to private life until 1802, when Étienne and Martainville rediscovered him in their book on the theater.[37]

The celebrations of Labussière that followed his rediscovery were multimedia: press, painting, theater. The tax farmers responsible for Comédie-Française's production of *Hamlet* pledged one-tenth of their share of the proceeds to the former clerk. "We see with pleasure," they wrote, that the actors were at last "acquitting the debt of recognition that the majority of them owe you for having included them in the great number of people who you saved from the revolutionary axe."[38] After the play, Labussière expressed his gratitude to all involved in a letter published in the theatrical newspaper the *Courrier des spectacles*:

> During this bloody period, horrible to remember, I had the pleasure of saving many victims from the revolutionary axe, at the risk of my life. How happy I would have been if this had not also involved the cruel necessity of risking the lives, more than once, of my comrades in the Prisoners Bureau, where I was hired as a copy clerk. I used a stratagem as simple as it was bizarre! I avow that without their courageous humanity, all of my efforts would have been useless. They unofficially closed their eyes to my thefts and, through their silence, associated themselves with the glories and dangers of my enterprises. The tigers that drank the blood of men, although seized by fear and suspicion, were not careful enough to suspect me. My neglected exterior and my frank and joking tone gave me an air of simplicity that made me seem unimportant in their eyes. I dared to be human in an era where humanity was a crime, and I arrived at saving an infinite number of people whose names I did not know, 1,153 prisoners.[39]

The blood and hyperbole in this account belong to the post-Thermidor pornography of political violence, yet there was more to the letter than that. Wittingly or not, the clerk was contributing to his own mythologization by casting himself as a figure from

French folklore. Étienne and Martainville had described him as a "simple employee." The author of the letter to the *Journal des Débats* had referred to him as a "simple individual." Labussière was now calling attention to his own "air of simplicity," to his "stratagem as simple as it was bizarre." This was no simple simplicity, however. It was the duplicitous simplicity of the trickster, which Robert Darnton notes is a "master theme" of eighteenth-century French culture.[40] This simple clerk had thwarted the most powerful men in France, relying on his cunning alone. While everyone else was looking *through* the files for orders or for information, he looked *at* them and recognized them for what they really were: ink and paper. With their fearsome deployment of paperwork and political violence, the members of the Committee of Public Safety represented a new kind of villain. They had been humiliated by an old kind of hero.

This trickster trope would be spun ad nauseam in the 1804 biography *Charles, ou Mémoires historiques de M. de la Bussière, ex-employé au Comité de Salut Public.*[41] The police official who was obliged to read it before publication was alarmed by its glamorous depictions of state sabotage. "This infidelity, no matter what one calls it, would still be unworthy of an honest man," he wrote in his report. He took solace in the fact that "the work is too miserable to produce any dangerous effects on public tranquility."[42] The book opened with a letter from the author to Labussière explaining how he had happened upon a manuscript containing various anecdotes about the clerk's life and was waiting only for his permission to see it into print. Labussière replied that he had no interest whatsoever in the matter; the author was free to do as he pleased. The biography then recounted Labussière's life in four small volumes of treacly prose. He had been born in 1768 to an ennobled family protected at court by the famously ill-fated Princesse de Lamballe. His greatest passion was the theater, and by the 1780s, he was taking part in small productions in Paris. The Revolution provided him with a new opportunity for acting out: he would disrupt section meetings by introducing absurd motions; he would attract large audiences in the gardens of the Palais-Royal by denouncing the latest conspiracy to steal—he would reveal once the suspense had built sufficiently—his hand-kerchief. These stories always concluded with his narrow escape from the humiliated sans-culotte mobs.

The book does not explain how Labussière ended up work-ing for the Committee of Public Safety, except to tell us that his friends, concerned that he was endangering himself with his street-theater antics, arranged for the position. Like Lejeune, he initially refused the offer. Once he arrived, though, he discovered that many of his coworkers felt much as he did. He noticed, for example, "that every time the bureau chief received orders to send documents, tears rolled down his cheeks, and often, under the pretext of a headache or terrible migraine, he would cover his face with his hands, look down at the desk, and cry."[43] This man was Fabien Pillet, who after the Revolution would become one of Labussière's foremost advocates. It was Pillet who suggested to Labussière that "the occupations of the employees, far from harming the unfortunate detainees, can help them. This office is nothing, and yet it is a lot." Nothing because, to all appearances, it was simply a brief stop for a small number of the documents circulating within the revolutionary government. A lot because "we can sometimes suspend the voracious activities of the Revo-lutionary Tribunal by working slowly and multiplying obstruc-tions. At the slightest pretext we can delay, as long as possible, the transfer of documents to the Popular Commission. This way we give the detainees time to have their relatives or friends intervene by bribing committee members who are the absolute masters over the lives of men."[44]

On May 11, 1794, the biography tells us, the clerk removed the first six documents. Over the following days, he removed sixty more. He acted cautiously at first. "But once experience had shown him how little order the commission placed in collecting its documents, he resolved to work on a grander scale." The biog-raphy explains in greater detail than ever before his procedure.

He would put the files of those who he had determined to save in a drawer that he then locked with a key. Every three or four days, he would return to the offices very late at night, flashing his entry card, and grope his way through the darkness to his desk. He would soak the files in the bucket of water kept there to cool the lunchtime wine. After pocketing the pulp, he would proceed to the nearby Vigier Baths, the large floating bathhouse at the bottom of the Pont Royal, where he would finish the deed. "These ingenious methods were the only ones possible during these times of rigorous surveillance," the biography assures the reader, "because burning the documents was impractical, especially during the heat of summer, when fire would seem unnecessary or suspect; because transporting the documents in their natural state would have been imprudent, given their volume and the guards' strict orders."[45] As for the final shredding of the documents in the public baths, it was necessary because the larger pellets dried quickly in the summer heat and might float to the top of the Seine, exposing his sabotage. By mid-June, Labussière had disposed of eight hundred files. By the end of June, he had rescued the French theater. And by the end of July, it was over. Labussière resigned from the Committee of Public Safety after making sure to "efface even the slightest traces of his hard work."[46]

Was it true? François-Alphonse Aulard, the first great archival historian of the French Revolution, professor at the Sorbonne, editor of the weighty twenty-eight-volume edition of the selected acts of the Committee of Public Safety, thought not. In 1891, during a revival of interest in Labussière coinciding with the revolutionary centennial, he dismissed the clerk as an "ingenious mystifier" and an "extortionist." He pointed to discrepancies in the biography, which were easy enough to find, but ultimately based his argument on his experience and credibility as a professional historian. "I would add that, having lived for years in the middle of the papers of the Committee of Public Safety, which I have undertaken to publish, this committee seems to me to have always maintained a habit for meticulous order and a tendency toward extreme simplification of paperwork."[47] In such an environment, Labussière would never have had the opportunity to delay, divert, or destroy files undetected.

It was a damning judgment, though perhaps not as final as it seemed to be. It would soon come to light that Aulard, misled by the existence of multiple, conflicting registers, had overlooked thousands of documents in his research, including those of the Prisoners Bureau.[48] Unfortunately, these archives do not settle the question, either. There appear to be no traces of Labussière's activities inside the offices of the Committee of Public Safety, except for the payroll records confirming that he was hired when he said he was hired and worked where he said he worked.[49] In the end, whether he was an ingenious mystifier remains an open question. That he was an ingenious demystifier, however, is beyond a doubt. Labussière revealed the vulnerability at the basis of the national-security state. Not only was power resistible, it was water soluble.

Matter, Form, and Power

By ensuring the surveillance and acceleration of the administration, the Committee of Public Safety was supposed to put an end to the chronic deferrals and displacements that prevented the full and prompt execution of the Republic's political will. It was meant to establish, in other words, a much longed-for immediacy, presence, and plenitude of sovereignty against the dangerous supplementarity of paperwork. The founding of the revolutionary dictatorship, its institutionalization with the law of 14 Frimaire (December 4), and the formation of the Bureau for Administrative Surveillance and General Police all followed this same impulse. Still, France remained vulnerable to paperwork's tedium and unpredictability.

Despite the opportunism that runs through their accounts, Lindet, Carnot, Lejeune, and Labussière all attest to the effects of the demon of writing, including the most enigmatic effect of all, the agency effect. With the power of life and death—sovereignty itself—seeming to have been corrupted and corroded by the committee's reliance on paperwork, the political relation between men had taken the form of a material relation between things, a distressing phenomenon that French dictionaries, at the end the eighteenth century, were only just beginning to call "bureaucracy."[50] This material relation did not simply eliminate individual agency, however. Rather, it refracted agency through its medium. Thus, Lindet and Carnot wanted to believe, or at least wanted it to be believed, that it was physically impossible to do otherwise than they had done. The combined but contradictory imperatives of surveillance and acceleration resulted in far too much paperwork needing to be completed far too quickly for there to be proper consideration of the political and moral consequences of any one signature. But Lejeune's and especially Labussière's stories would illustrate the flaws in this defense, one that has since become sadly familiar.[51] The materiality of paperwork in fact presented unmistakable opportunities for resistance to the terrorist regime through everyday strategies of deferral and displacement; its superabundance meant that such opportunities presented themselves over and over again.

The most reliable account of Labussière's later years was provided by Fabien Pillet, his friend, supervisor, and possible accomplice. Writing the entry for Michaud's *Biographie universelle* in the 1840s, Pillet described how the benefit performance of *Hamlet* had raised fourteen thousand francs for the former clerk.

> But unable to economize, Labussière soon dissipated this sum, and despite the secret aid of the Empress Josephine, via the hands of Madame de la Rouchefoucauld, he fell into a state of extreme misery. Following a violent attack of paralysis, his intellectual faculties became so deranged that the police were forced to keep him locked up in a madhouse, where he died soon after, entirely forgotten even by those for whom he most risked his life.[52]

(Pillet himself went on to become a noted arts critic, dying in 1855. Of his own revolutionary experience, the Michaud mentions

74

only that he had "the good fortune to pass unnoticed during the reign of terror.")[53]

The trickster lived on, however, in national mythology. Alexandre Dumas *père* was said to have considered turning his story into a novel.[54] The task fell instead to Jules Claretie, who incorporated Labussière into his revolutionary potboiler *Puyjoli*. Published as France celebrated the Revolution's centennial, the novel emphasized the moral conundrum of Labussière's actions. "One scruple stopped him: To violate the law! It was the law, law of marble, venerated, a sovereign goddess reigning. The law! And brows furrowed. The law! And armed men dropped their weapons. The law! And the nation responded, I will obey." How could a simple clerk dare defy it? "Above human law, eh! citizen—there is Humanity!"[55]

Claretie's novel was soon followed by his fellow academician Victorien Sardou's play *Thermidor*, which had to be shut down after opening night when protestors, led by Hippolyte-Prosper-Olivier Lissagaray—the great chronicler of the Paris Commune and greatly frustrated suitor of Eleanor Marx—objected to what he perceived to be criticisms of the Revolution.[56] It was during the parliamentary debates over whether to ban the play from the French stage that Clemenceau made his famous speech declaring "The Revolution is a bloc," providing a slogan for republican historiography for the next century. Censored in France, the play traveled abroad, including to New York, where a condescending editorial in the *New York Times* offered the episode as yet another example of French politics gone awry.[57] The ban was finally lifted in 1894; a restaurant on the Boulevard Saint-Denis celebrated reopening night by placing on its menu a new culinary creation, lobster Thermidor.[58]

Twentieth-century variations of this myth range from a biography published in England under the title *A Whoreson Mad Fellow*, to an essay by the Polish director Zygmunt Hubner, to an entry in the French-language Wikipedia. One version, though, stands out above the rest, Abel Gance's cinematic bio-epic *Napoléon* of 1927 (see figures 4 and 5).[59] The scene featuring Labussière opens with a shot of files stacked to the ceiling inside the offices of the Committee of Public Safety. A man suspended from a rope apparatus travels up and down the towering shelves, retrieving dossiers, which he passes to a clerk who is ordered to hurry: there must be three hundred heads a day. The camera then pulls back to reveal a cluttered, chaotic office. The clerk scurries to his desk and sets to work, quill in hand. He soon comes across a dossier with the name Josephine de Beauharnais, the future empress. The camera closes in as he looks around to make sure he is not being observed, then bites into it, laboriously chewing, swallowing, and digesting the pages. The clerk next to him watches in wonder and then follows his lead, soon devouring the dossier for Napoleon Bonaparte. "Happily, Labussière watches over them, this strange character who, out of humanity, became a thief of dossiers," an intertitle tells us. "Not a thief, but a chewer, risking his life at every instant to save the lives of unknowns."[60] In the film, Labussière's heroism becomes a founding moment in the history of France.

CHAPTER THREE

The State of Want

The first appearance of the word "bureaucracy" (*la bureaucratie*) in print was in a July 1764 issue of Melchior von Grimm's *Correspondance littéraire*, the biweekly newsletter of arts, letters, and politics whose subscription list included some of the most powerful names in Europe.[1] Celebrating recent advances in the liberalization of the French grain trade, the author took a moment to remember the late Vincent de Gournay, who, as mentor to Turgot and the Physiocratic movement, had helped popularize the principle of "laissez-faire," a phrase that he also coined.[2] Grimm recounted how Gournay had once remarked to him that "'we have in France an illness that takes a terrible toll; this illness is called bureaumania.'" He even described this mania as "a fourth or fifth form of government, by the name of bureaucracy."[3]

This new word "bureaucracy" simultaneously invoked and violated a well-worn semiotic code. To the classic three regimes, democracy, aristocracy, and monarchy—that is, rule by the many, the few, and the one—Gournay had now added rule by a piece of office furniture. This piece of furniture was expandable, metonymically, to include the men who sat behind it, the offices in which they found themselves, and ultimately the entire state apparatus. More than an ordinary neologism, "bureaucracy" was a pun, a "rattling of the semiotic chain," as Lacan says. Sarcasm, satire, and related genres emerge out of a relationship between subjects. The pun emerges out of the subject's relationship to language, to culture, to what Lacan calls the "Other." "The essence of the pun—if we want to search for it, and search for it with Freud, since he will take it as far as possible in the direction of its point, and it really is a question of a point, there is a point—consists in a radical relationship to the truth."[4]

What truth? Not some metaphysical "truth" of the state—its secret class nature, as the Marxists have argued, or even the fact that it often gets its facts wrong, as James C. Scott has shown—so much as the truth of a desire that modern individuals have both directed and misdirected at the state for the last quarter-millennium or so. This is a desire that surpasses a basic need for safety, prosperity, and other more or less tangible goods. It even exceeds the forms of recognition that many of us, especially racial, religious, and sexual minorities, have demanded of the state. Such needs can be met; such demands can be fulfilled. It is the nature of desire, however, to be unfulfillable. The story of "bureaucracy"—all of our jokes, anecdotes, complaints, even our occasional stories of triumph—is a story of this desire that is not reducible to a need or demand. It is the story of how paperwork, even when it works, fails us. We never get what we want.

We observed this in miniature in the first chapter. In the beginning, all Edme-Etienne Morizot wanted was his job back. This basic need slowly transformed itself into a more complicated demand for recognition by the new state—recognition of his suffering, his sacrifices, his worth. By the end, he was after something that neither a job nor an apology could have provided, though they sure would have been nice. What we find in stories such as Morizot's are not struggles for resources or recognition so much as a struggle for satisfaction. A satisfaction that both theoretical wisdom and historical evidence suggest is insatiable. A satisfaction that may or may not be articulate or even articulable. A satisfaction that is often, maybe even always, essentially unavailable to even the most sympathetic and imaginative historian. Indeed, it would be a serious mistake to assume that we know too much about what others in history—or even the others we read about in this morning's newspaper—want. For the purposes of this chapter, it will be enough to know that they do want, that like us, they live in a state of want, and that like us, they seek explanations for why they can't get what they want. When we can't get our wants met, we at least want an explanation. Our endless, repetitive stories about "bureaucracy" are the form that explanation takes in the modern world. These stories, the pleasure we take in sharing them with one another, are often the closest we will ever get—as historians, critical theorists, and citizens—to obtaining satisfaction from the state.

Did Grimm's readers laugh? Smirk? Groan? There is no way of knowing for sure. What we do know is that in 1750, the word "bureaucracy" was nowhere; by 1850, it was everywhere. While once-common invectives such as "ministerial despotism" all but disappeared, funny or plaintive or funny-plaintive stories about "bureaucracy" flourished, spreading from France to England and Germany and, eventually, around the world, transcending national, linguistic, and even ideological boundaries. The primary vehicles for the term's dissemination were not political or philosophical treatises, but popular literature. It is for this reason, I think, that even those historians of political thought most attentive to the role of language—members of the Cambridge School, say—have tended to miss the emergence of "bureaucracy" as a master signifier, surely one of the most spectacular linguistic-conceptual success stories of the modern era. Writers and readers turned to popular print culture to experiment with this very literal manifestation of what Slavoj Žižek has called "enjoyment as a political factor."[5] Because of its intimate relationship to this conflicted, symptomatic pleasure, literature was always one or two steps ahead of philosophy or sociology when it came to understanding the powers and failures of paperwork. For better or for worse, nineteenth-century writers such as Alexis de Tocqueville would find themselves turning to literature to refresh their theories of the state.

79

Writing and Indifference

One might have expected Gournay's pun to catch on immediately as men and women throughout the Enlightenment public sphere struggled to secure a domain of activity independent of state intervention. Even those writers who remained unconvinced by protoliberal arguments such as Gournay's were frequently unhappy with the intrusions of royal authority into their everyday actions and transactions. However, there are almost no other instances of "bureaucracy" in print before the French Revolution. It may be that few readers came into contact with the word, since the circulation of Grimm's *Correspondance littéraire* was so limited. It may also be that nobody thought Gournay's pun was worth repeating.

Indeed, the word "bureaucracy" might have disappeared from the lexicon altogether had it not been either reinvented or rediscovered—it is not clear which—in the final months of the Old Regime. In 1788, Louis-Sebastien Mercier, the chronicler of Parisian life and letters, explained in his *Tableau de Paris* that "bureaucracy" was "a word recently coined to indicate, in a clear and concise manner, the overgrown power possessed by simple clerks who, in the various offices of the administration, make up and push forward all sorts of projects, which they find most often in dusty drawers in the offices, and which they favor for reasons of their own, good or bad." These men, he added, "are all the more powerful with their pens because their actions are never visible."[6] He elaborated on this theme in another article in the *Tableau de Paris*, "Plumes de commis." The nation was menaced by an "innumerable race of quill sharpeners, assessing, calculating, using cursive and italic letters." What would Charlemagne have thought, he asked, of these "regiments of scribblers who immortalize a payment of twelve sols, who record the entry of a rabbit into the city, and who, when a bottle of wine appears, sign and initial a tax receipt with the date and location?"[7]

Mercier's critique condenses and displaces multiple contemporary anxieties about the technics of power. But one anxiety

stands out as more severe than all the rest: the proximity of clerks
to paperwork invested them with a degree of power completely
out of proportion to their social and political status. As paperwork took on more and more importance in the revolutionary
decade, this anxiety would become ever more acute. Not long
after Mercier's definition of "bureaucracy" appeared in the *Tableau de Paris*, for example, the *Encyclopédie méthodique* included an
article on the subject by Jacques Peuchet, a well-respected liberal
political economist who had occupied a number of important
positions in the administration.[8] For Peuchet, the phenomenon
of "bureaucracy" (which he spelled *burocratie*) was "an abuse as
bizarre as it is incredible" that arose when "bureaus meant to play
a subaltern role set themselves up as magistrates, exempting this
or that person from submission to the laws or subjecting citizens
to obligations which they reject. It is administration when corrupt or stupid clerks set themselves up as ministers, turning the
public fortune into an object for personal speculation, changing,
reforming, altering the best regulations, suspending or stopping
useful establishments, etc." It is, above all, "command when the
agents of sovereign power accept orders from men incompetent
to give them."[9]

Such critiques of "bureaucracy"—first sketched out in the
months leading up to the Revolution—would allow for an articu-
lation between essentially democratic concerns about the legitimacy of power and essentially liberal concerns about the status
of civil society. As we know, this link between liberal and democratic concerns was neither necessary nor obvious in the late
eighteenth century. (It would become much more obvious in the
nineteenth and twentieth centuries, though no more necessary.)
A shared opposition to "bureaucracy" enabled these inconsistent
and even contradictory political sensibilities to work together
as friends against a common enemy. The term became a vague
expression of an even vaguer sense that something, or someone,
or many someones—anyone or anything but the structural contradictions of the liberal-democratic project as such—had to be to

blame for how much paperwork was required not only to govern, but to be governed in the modern world.

The disavowal was necessary because this truth was, in fact, extremely troubling, even traumatic. Not only did the proliferation of paperwork contradict normative principles about the relationship between the state and civil society, the state and the citizen, it made life hard. Total strangers suddenly had a strange and total power over you. This dissemination of power by paperwork was perceived as fundamentally unreasonable at a moment when appeals to reason had special force. Jan Goldstein has shown how accusations of insanity, particularly mania, functioned in French political culture of the era. One of four basic types of insanity recognized in the late eighteenth century—along with frenzy, melancholy, and imbecility—mania turned its sufferers into what Esquirol called "the very picture of chaos, whose moving elements collide with and contradict one another incessantly."[10] Starting with Grimm's allusion to "bureaumania," the idea that the state had become manic was an important trope. "This mania for the quill, which dates to Monsieur Colbert, has only reached such a scandalous degree over the last three years," Mercier wrote in an article in *Le Nouveau Paris* (1798–99). "Clerks, papers, details have absorbed everything."[11]

Little wonder liberalism was so unsettled. In Frimaire Year II, for example, the editors of the *La Décade Philosophique* published a letter under the title "Bureaucratic Moeurs." Though the letter was unsigned, the historian R. R. Palmer has argued that it was almost certainly written by the liberal political economist Jean-Baptiste Say, one of the journal's editors, possibly to fill out a thinner than usual issue.[12] "Have you not sometimes had to deal with public functionaries who abuse the preeminence over you that comes with their position and your need for them? Who treat you, with their words and actions, in a way that they would never permit themselves to be treated if they needed something from you?" Say opened his letter. "It is this kind of abuse that I am writing to denounce."[13]

The letter then launched into a story of a friend who had left Paris for his native region to get married, only to find that he had overlooked a crucial bit of paperwork before his departure: he was supposed to post a marriage announcement in his Paris neighborhood. Rectifying the oversight would mean waiting three days while his request traveled to Paris, three more days while the public exercised its right to register any objections to the posting, and then another three days for a certificate to travel back from Paris with proof of his compliance. The friend wrote Say in desperation, asking if there was any way he could hasten things. Eager to help, Say posted the marriage announcement, returning three days later to get the document that attested to the fulfillment of all formal obligations.

He arrived on time for his appointment, only to be left waiting while the commissioner, pretending to ignore his presence, arranged and rearranged the items on his desk. This is when things got interesting. Just as it seemed that Say was about to receive the paperwork he needed, the commissioner's daughter-in-law entered the office wearing nothing but a filthy negligee. She had heard a song out on the street and wanted pen and paper to record it immediately. Alas, there was only one functioning pen in the entire office. Say was left waiting while the young woman, who also made a point of ignoring him, wrote out the music and lyrics. He waited some more while the commissioner resharpened the quill's nib. Finally, the time had come. "I took a deep breath," Say writes. "I needed only two lines and his signature." At that very moment, the commissioner's servant arrived at the office with packages of beef and mutton, which any reader would have recognized as symbols of luxury. Say remained there, biting his tongue, while the public servant and the public servant's servant debated the best way to prepare the meat. At last, an hour and a half after his scheduled appointment, Say received his two lines and a signature. "In a Republic, to waste the time of a citizen this way! A person who is supposed to be nothing more than the employee of the people! paid by them!"[14]

On the one hand, Say's letter was a straightforward exercise in a comic genre: insolent servants, dimwitted daughters. On the other hand, it is a story of how a simple chore could become a much more complex search for something less certain, less obtainable, but no less compelling—in fact, all the more compelling because of its uncertainty, its unobtainability. "Comedy is the permanent suspension, postponement, or parody of catharsis," Simon Critchley notes in a gloss of Lacan's seminar on the ethics of psychoanalysis. "Comedy is the eruption of materiality into the spiritual purity of tragic action and desire."[15] The serious work of the Republic is interrupted by daughters and dinner plans, but more importantly by the materiality of communication: the two lines and a signature that are simultaneously the path toward the satisfaction of desire (in this case figured quite literally as the friend's nuptials) and the obstacle to any such satisfaction. Say leaves as he came: in a state of want. He can never get his time back.

Even very serious—and very illiberal—writers could take some pleasure in this genre. In his *Theory of Power* (1796), for example, Louis de Bonald alluded back to Vincent de Gournay. "France, according to a man of wit, was neither an aristocracy nor a democracy, but a bureaucracy." The same could be said of the modern state:

> this bureaucratic mania has even infiltrated the military: commanders, high officers spend all their time writing or signing status reports. These functions absorb a man, restrict his mind; the extreme attention paid to things makes attention to people nearly impossible. Small-mindedness and a mania for details have won out in France to the point where a young soldier could teach even the most skilled housewife a thing or two about how to bake bread, tailor shirts, keep accounts.[16]

The comic tone is crucial here, because it defuses the potentially radical insight into the alienation of clerical labor. The rhetoric of "bureaucracy" simultaneously raised the possibility of critique and contained it within the boundaries of a popular genre.

Looking back over the revolutionary decade in *Le Nouveau Paris*, Mercier observed that paperwork had increased "with such profusion and such little discernment" that many citizens had simply given up on the state, deciding to do without pensions and other services. The most insignificant clerk in the most distant locale "is surrounded by more bundles of paper, more affairs, than the Minister of War ever was under the Old Regime. With the quill one governs everything, without appeal." Across France, "papers and bureaus multiply to infinity. The people who handle the details need clerks, the clerks need copyists, the copyists need office boys, and this is subdivided still further." This relentless division of labor had brought thousands of inept employees into the government, "a crowd of fools, ignoramuses, traitors, and royalists who have mistaken their hunger for zeal, and their zeal for talent.... You will say that I am exaggerating, but the spelling errors, the grammatical errors, the errors of meaning are the least of the vices of these young marvels who were formerly so despicable." Mercier, who had been imprisoned in the Terror for his political moderation, could not possibly have been unaware of the violence of his language. "It is time," he concluded, to "clean up the administrations, the agencies, the commissions, the committees of all their trash."[17]

In 1798, the Académie française added "bureaucracy" to its dictionary: "Power, influence of bureau chiefs and clerks in the Administration."[18] This was a modest entry for a term with such mythopoetic potential. In his invaluable survey of French state formation since the Revolution, referring to the early uses of the term, Pierre Rosanvallon writes that the "humor attests to the impotence of the French to seize intellectually the increase of bureaucracy in the modern world. The pathological and satirical approach to the problem allows the sociological dimension not to be analyzed."[19] But this perhaps misinterprets the nature and function of the joke-work performed by these writings. The stories about "bureaucracy" are not the sign of a failure of intellection; they are one of the forms that intellection takes. This would become ever clearer in the nineteenth century, when authors would turn to the comedy of "bureaucracy" to produce some of the most serious thinking about the state.

"Women and White Paper"

It was only after the end of the Napoleonic period that state satire emerged definitively in France.[20] The defeat of the Empire, with its routine censorship of political criticism, was followed by a rapid expansion and diversification of the literary marketplace.[21] Two contradictions in Restoration political culture converged to feed the interest in "bureaucracy" within this new marketplace. First, the restored monarchy, though increasingly backward-looking ideologically, maintained most of the administrative structures built over the previous quarter-century—François Furet remarks that Louis XVIII was simultaneously "the lord of lords and the head of a modern administration."[22] Second, the rapid change in regimes had involved a series of administrative purges, leaving a number of highly literate men with the time finally to write that first novel they had always been talking about.[23]

One such man was Jacques-Gilbert Ymbert. His biography offers us a glimpse into the life of an ambitious and successful civil servant in the revolutionary era. One of fourteen children, he was born in Paris in 1786 to a petit-bourgeois family soon ruined by the Revolution. But he did well in school and at the age of twenty entered the Ministry of War as a *surnuméraire*, essentially an intern. A year later, he was promoted to *commis titulaire*, and four years after that to *sous-chef de bureau*. In 1814, he became *chef de bureau* in the Division of Conscription, a post that he held into the First Restoration, only to be purged in 1816 for having allied himself with Napoleon during the Hundred Days. Two years later, he was rehired as a lowly *commis* and then promoted to *sous-chef* before being purged again in 1822 for sympathizing with the liberal opposition. From 1822 to 1827, he directed a private insurance fund against conscription while using his spare time to write about life in the bureaus. After the July Revolution, he reentered the government at the highest levels: first as secretary-general of the Office of Inspection of the National Guard, then as *maître des requêtes* for the Conseil d'État, and finally as a division chief in the Ministry of the Interior.[24]

Ymbert would be just one nineteenth-century observer among others—a lesser Eugène Sue, with whom he sometimes collabo-rated—were it not for the fact that his 1825 treatise *Les moeurs administratives* was understood by many of his contemporaries to be the most reliable source for inside knowledge about the inner workings of the French administration. Writing in *Le Mercure du dix-neuvième siècle*, where the book had been partly serialized, the critic Philarète Chasles enthused that "everything is on display in this work.... No vague systems, no generalizations. Everything is positive, real, based on experience. He tells us how things happen, how the millions flood from this administrative Marly machine, turning into waves of ink." Chasles, who obviously enjoyed his own prose at least as much as Ymbert's, promoted the book as a portrait of "man submitted to bureaucratic discipline, man become a piece of writing furniture, a telegraph of admin-istration, without thought, without will, without existence."[25] Meanwhile, the June 1826 issue of the *Edinburgh Review* offered its readers numerous excerpts from Ymbert's book as the basis of a long reflection on French politics and culture. "We shall here close notice of this work," the reviewer concluded, "with the expression of our sincere wish, that France may be half as suc-cessful in obtaining the blessings of our form of Government, as she has evidently been in copying its corruptions and defects."[26]

Some sense of Ymbert's basic position can be gained from an entry on "bureaucracy" that he wrote for Courtin's *Encyclopédie moderne*. "The revolution, in destroying and rebuilding, often found the dictionary too impoverished to describe its ruins and its constructions," he wrote. "It was necessary to have recourse to new words to provide for new circumstances." In Ymbert's ety-mology, the word "bureaucracy" was originally a value-neutral term designating the new institutions that emerged out of the revolutionary decade. However, "minds that had long been accustomed to finding power only in the hands of a small number of men who passed it along from father to son were terrified by the appearance of this tribe of employees, which had previously, in the former order of things, been hidden." Moreover, "the numerous promotions, destitutions, and acts of violence to which this personnel were subjected by governments, as they were established or overthrown, brought this new mode of administration into discredit." The result was that the word "bureaucracy" was transformed from a neutral term into a term of abuse, "today expressing nothing more than the overabundance of employees, the surplus of positions, the abuse of sinecures, and the dangerous centralization of power in hands that use it to serve their personal fortunes and ambitions."[27]

Ymbert's article was thus a vigorous defense of his coworkers against the vicious attacks of the politicians and press. Operating a modern constitutional state was expensive. To provide services, the state must collect and redistribute taxes. This was made possible by a large body of dedicated personnel. It was simply absurd "to declaim against these unfortunate agents who, under a thousand different forms and a thousand different names, work for three francs a day in order to bring into the treasury the piles of gold that you divide between force, luxury, laziness, and crazy prodigality. You want those piles of gold? Then you also want bureaucracy." In Ymbert's article, "bureaucracy" properly understood is "a necessity, a complement to constitutional government."[28]

Readers might well have found it hard to reconcile this argument with the more sensational revelations contained in Ymbert's book *Les moeurs administratives*, which took the form of a collection of epistles to an unidentified female correspondent. "The administration overruns everything," he warns breathlessly in the book's preface. "Administrators swarm, and still ninety-nine percent of the population is completely unaware of the nature of this driving force that, pushing us ahead with ordinances, regulations,

and decrees, constrains us to walk straight along the grand road
of obedience."[29] The treatise opens by recounting, in a humor-
ous tone, the story of the social contract. When you say "I am
French," he asks his reader, what does that mean? It means "I am
part of a nation composed of more than thirty million individuals" who have agreed to "sacrifice a portion of their natural liberty and money in order to live under the protection of collective
laws that guarantee each the peaceful enjoyment of the remainder
of his goods and faculties." To execute laws, to maintain collective security, one needs a king. But the king cannot "hear thirty
million voices, nor administer alone the portion of natural liberty
and money sacrificed by the thirty million subjects." Other ears
and other hands are needed to collect taxes, conduct foreign relations, resolve domestic disturbances, punish thieves, make rivers
navigable, construct bridges, erect monuments, and maintain
the hospitals. "This is how we got the ministries of finance, war,
justice, and the interior."[30]

Such administration was not in and of itself problematic. But
there was a disturbing tendency toward excess. In addition to
these indispensable ministries were the extraneous ones: "the
ministries of religion, commerce, etc."[31] This *luxe administratif*
was the true source of France's difficulties. Each of these ministries added to the king's two hands the two hands of the minister,
plus thirty to forty thousand more—each of which is salaried,
Ymbert explains, with the money and liberty sacrificed by the
French subject in hope of obtaining some security and well-being.
Once the state exceeded a certain number of hands, it could no
longer guarantee that each one knew what the other was doing.
Ymbert depicts the resulting disarray over hundreds of pages. His
tour of the ministries leads down corridors, through offices, and
past clerks studying the violin, taking English lessons, composing
skits, building models, stitching clothes—everything, apparently,
but doing their jobs.

Some of the letters are quite eloquent on the place of paperwork and the plight of paperworkers. "The fate of all petitions is

to expire in the hands of a clerk assigned to its area," he explains to his correspondent in "Letter Eight."

> Do you want clemency for a guilty person, exemption from a tax, fodder for the cavalry? Your petition will inevitably arrive at the desk of an employee in the offices of Monseigneur Keeper of the Seals, or Their Eminences the Ministers of Finance and War. Have it written by an academician or by a member of a literary society; send it on the silkiest vellum via the loveliest hands; ask a Peer of France to deliver it personally to the minister. Or simply drop it in the post—its fate will be the same.[32]

Sooner or later, your petition would end up in the hands of a clerk. The fancier the path, the longer the wait. "Petitions all resemble water flowing downhill: you can start them off as high as you like, but eventually they will trickle down into the vast bureaucratic ocean."[33]

Nor was it only citizens who had to endure such delays.

> Each day, a thousand dispatches, parting from a thousand different places, are addressed to each minister. You suppose that the first order of business, once they arrive, is to read them, to take note of their content? Not at all: the most important thing is to record on each letter a number for the registers. This is the responsibility of one or several clerks who do not believe that a letter to the minister can exist until it has received from their hands what we call an order number.[34]

Imagine a prefect or general writing to the minister of war with an urgent request for troops, Ymbert tells us.

> The head of the Mail Bureau opens the packet that carries this life-or-death request. His rested, relaxed eyes see only a piece of paper beginning, like all the others, with the customary *monseigneur*, and concluding with the *j'ai l'honneur d'être avec un profond respect*. He carefully places it in order, sharpens his quill, puts on his glasses, and slowly registers the 999 letters that preceded it. Finally, when

and only when it is the letter's turn, he applies the obligatory order number. If some hasty or troublesome hand tries to take the letter before it has been duly registered, the head of the Mail Bureau cries anarchy, usurpation, an overturning of all ideas of order. You think that by the time he has sharpened his quill, put on his glasses, registered and numbered the letter, the insurrection will have won. Never fear: Only the town of Thouars has fallen, although if administrative custom required two numbers instead of one, no doubt Saumur would also be lost.[35]

Balzac would turn to Ymbert's letters while researching and writing the novel that would eventually become *Les employés, ou La femme supérieure*. Like many of his texts, this novel has a complicated publishing history. The basic story was first serialized as "La femme supérieure" in *La Presse* in July 1837; it was then reprinted, with relatively few modifications, in book form in 1838. A third version, integrating long sections from yet another of his texts, "La physiologie de l'employé," then appeared in 1844 as part of Furne's edition of *La comédie humaine*.[36]

This novel continued Balzac's exploration of modernity's "heroic potential."[37] In fact, the novel can be interpreted as an explicit answer to the implicit question whether heroism can exist at all within the French administration. The answer is divided into three parts. The novel's first part, entitled "Between Two Women," introduces the readers to the book's central struggle, namely, the competition between two bureau chiefs, aided by their wives, for promotion to division chief. Xavier Rabourdin is a serious, scrupulous reformer; his wife, Célestine, is intelligent and ambitious, a "superior woman," in the words of the novel's original title. Isidore Baudoyer, their opponent, is "simply a bureaucrat"; his wife, Élisabeth, "is one of those figures who escape portraiture through their total ordinariness." The middle part of the novel, "The Bureaus," describes the setting in which this contest will take place—an anonymous Restoration ministry with a dying division chief circa 1824. The hero's disgrace and defeat occur in the final part, "To Whom the Place?"[38]

Closely following Ymbert, Balzac argued that the French Revolution had brought about a transformation in the status and function of state employees: "Formerly, under the monarchy, the bureaucratic armies did not exist," he writes near the beginning of the book. "Few in number, the clerks were under the orders of a prime minister who was always in communication with the sovereign; thus they directly served the king." But the French Revolution had put an end to this way of doing things. Since 1789, "the State, or the *patrie*, if you like, has replaced the Prince." The clerks no longer depend directly on the king or his prime minister; instead, they are "employees of the government." Thus emboldened, Balzac laments, these clerks have proceeded to "substitute written action for living action" by creating "a power of inertia called the Report." In France, "nothing important happens in the administration without the minister responding, even in the most urgent cases, 'I have requested a report.'" It was ruining the nation. "No matter what you do, the moment comes when the decision must be made," he insists. "The more one weighs the reasons for and against, the less sound the judgment. The finest things in France were accomplished when reports did not exist and decisions were spontaneous." Under the Restoration, when the action described in the novel takes place, there were "a million reports each year! Thus did bureaucracy reign!"[39]

In Balzac's account, this postrevolutionary excess of paperwork and the ensuing confusion of power were only the beginning of the problem. The rot afflicted individuals, families, and finally the nation as a whole. Forced to deal with this influx of documents, ministers hired more and more clerks, lowering salaries to permit this expansion. The quality of the personnel diminished accordingly. "Occupied only with maintaining himself, receiving his salary, and obtaining his pension, the employee believed that anything was permitted." Furthermore, the civil equality established by the French Revolution had led a number of young men to lose sight of their station in life: the "sons of concierges" now felt entitled to decide the fate of even the most powerful. "The really useful people, the hard workers," became "victims of the parasites." "Certainly," he writes, "a country does not seem immediately menaced with death because a talented employee retires and is replaced by a mediocre one. Unfortunately for nations, no man appears to be indispensable to their existence. But when everything weakens over the long term, nations disappear."[40]

The novel opens as Rabourdin prepares to unveil a massive plan for the reform of the French administration, crafted over years of cautious observation and calculation. Balzac devotes a great deal of attention to the details of this plan; his manuscripts for the novel show that he worked on it carefully.[41] The plan entails "reorganizing taxes in such a way as to lower them without the state losing any revenue and obtaining, with a budget equal to that which was then causing so many crazy discussions, results that were twice as considerable as the current ones."[42] Why, for example, did there need to be separate ministries for war and the navy? The elimination of redundancies would permit a reduction in the number of personnel; this would in turn permit an improvement in working conditions, which would attract a better sort of person to the state and thus bring a better sort of state to the people. In this plan, "there was no employee who did not receive a large consideration, as merited by the extent of his labor."[43] Properly compensated, these men would serve the nation faithfully and diligently.

More interesting than this plan for reform are the descriptions of the man who presents it; there is a positive model of the bureaucrat that is missing from most contemporary texts. Balzac sums up his administrator-hero quickly, but precisely. He is

> philosophical enough to take life for what it was; an honest man who loved and served his country without dissimulating the obstacles that one encountered in wanting to do good; prudent because he knew men; exquisitely polite to women because he expected nothing from them; finally, a man full of knowledge, behaving affably to

his inferiors, keeping a great distance from his equals, and maintaining a high level of dignity with his chiefs.[44]

He is a modern figure, as distinct from the overly ambitious enlightened administrator of the Old Regime as he is from the murderously determined Jacobin official of the Year II. His plans are tempered by an awareness of the fallibility of all human endeavors, including his own. "What made Rabourdin truly great," Balzac writes, "was that he knew how to contain the enthusiasm that seizes all inventors, to search patiently for measures that would avoid shocks, allowing time and experience to demonstrate the excellence of each change."[45] He was the ideal figure of authority.

The contrast with the men who surround him is extreme. The novel contains particularly savage depictions of the clerks, chiefs, and high officials who thwart Rabourdin and his plan for reform. The personal secretary of the minister, for example, is compared to a poodle, a plant, a servant, a virgin, a whore, and white paper in a rapid series of quips:

> The Emperor of Russia would be thankful to be able to pay fifty thousand a year to one of these amiable constitutional poodles, so gentle, so nicely curled, so caressing, so docile, so well groomed, so attentive—and so faithful! But the private secretary only grows in the greenhouses of a representative government. Under the monarchy you have only courtesans and servants, whereas with a Charter you are served, flattered, and caressed by free men. Ministers, in France, are thus happier than women and kings—they have somebody who understands them. Perhaps we should pity these private secretaries like we pity women and white paper—they must bear everything. Like chaste women, they must only have secret talents, and only for their ministers. If they have talent in public, they are lost.[46]

Amid this metaphorical excess there is a certain moral ambivalence. On the one hand, Balzac finds these subjects deeply disturbing; not only do they do irreparable harm to the state, but they also undermine the hierarchies of class and gender that he sees as the very essence of the social order. On the other hand, he seems to recognize that they are also victims of circumstance and worthy of the reader's sympathy. He gestures toward the specific historical and material conditions that make life so difficult for these men, but he gestures rudely.

This ambivalence manifests itself most clearly in his description of the physical spaces in which clerks labor. "In Paris, nearly all bureaus resemble one another," Balzac writes. "In whichever ministry you wander into, for some small favor or for the rectification of some minor wrong, you will find dark corridors, poorly lighted stairwells, doors with . . . incomprehensible signs." The air is unbreathable because the chimney is blocked. The wallpaper is solid green or solid brown. Empty bottles and scraps of food are strewn about. Occasionally a bureau would have to be moved from one building to another. "Of all the relocations in Paris, the most grotesque are those of administrations. Even the genius of Hoffman, that bard of the impossible, never invented anything so fantastical." As the carriages pass with the furnishings, "the boxes yawn open leaving a tail of dust in the streets. Tables with their four legs in the air, overturned chairs, the unbelievable utensils with which France is administered—all have a terrifying physiognomy."[47] Confined within these cramped, uncanny spaces, the clerks spend their time looking for ways to amuse themselves (one, whose hobby is predicting the future with anagrams, discovers "un Corse la finira" in "Révolution française").[48] How could men spending eight or nine hours a day in such conditions not degenerate? "It is difficult to decide whether these plumed mammals were getting stupider because of their careers, or whether they had these careers because they were born stupid," Balzac writes. "Perhaps it is equal parts Nature and Government."[49]

In such a habitat, Rabourdin and his plan cannot take root. The division chief's dying wish is that he be replaced by Rabourdin, whom everyone agrees is worthier than Baudoyer, his rival for the office. But what should be a simple succession is complicated by the discovery, by one of the clerks from Baudoyer's office, of a particularly sensitive piece of Rabourdin's project: his written evaluations of the entire ministerial staff. Baudoyer's subordinates, when they discover this document, realize its value: if they can arrange for their chief to receive the promotion, then they, too, will have opportunities to advance up the office hierarchy. They thus decide to discredit Rabourdin. "In the end, are the offices not a microcosm of society, with their oddities, their friendships, their hatreds, their envy, and their cupidity, their relentless march forward, their frivolous conversations that inflict so many wounds, and their perpetual spying?"[50] Significantly, it is his commitment to paperwork that ensnares Balzac's hero. How could Rabourdin resist putting everything in writing, even at the risk of his livelihood?

The stern lecture that Célestine gives Xavier Rabourdin when she realizes his carelessness in writing down his plan articulates the fundamental pessimism about the possibilities of reform that determine the conclusion of the novel. He protests that she does not know all the details of his plan.

> "Do I need," she said, "to know a scheme whose essence is to administer France with six thousand employees instead of twenty thousand? But, my friend, even if it were the plan of a man of genius, a king of France would end up dethroned trying to execute it. One can defeat a feudal aristocracy by chopping off a few heads, but one does not defeat a hydra with a thousand legs. No, you cannot crush the little folk, they are too flat underfoot."[51]

The annotated list of government employees is furnished to the minister as proof that Rabourdin is "the agent of an unknown power for which he has done extensive espionage throughout the ministries." Rabourdin, the minister is told, "is organizing an entire government, without doubt on behalf of some secret society that we do not know."[52] Disgraced, Rabourdin must quit the government. When his realizes his fate, he announces a new plan to his wife: "I worked uselessly for my country, because I thought I could be useful to it...now I am going to take a different path.

If I had been a grocer, we would be millionaires. Very well, let's become grocers. You are only twenty-eight years old, my angel. Very well, in ten years, hard work will give you the luxury you love."[53] Disgusted by his state servitude, Balzac's hero decides to try to get what he wants from the world of commerce. It is Candide for the capitalist era: he will cultivate profit from somebody else's garden.

Is Tocqueville Kidding?

"Although it has passed into common usage to use 'bureaucracy' as an abstract designation for all those who administer, it is nevertheless modern jargon that we must try to avoid." Alexis de Tocqueville jotted this reminder to himself in the manuscripts of *The Old Regime and the Revolution*. And while he ended up using the word once in another chapter of the book—and one or two times elsewhere—for the most part, he successfully followed his own advice.

Or perhaps he was for the most part successfully following the advice of the Académie française, which took the unusual step of downgrading the term from written to spoken language in a usage note included in the 1835 edition of its dictionary: "This new word is employed exclusively in conversation, to express the abusive influence of clerks in the administration."[54] The note is somewhat difficult to interpret. It could not have been purely descriptive, since the word appeared in print all the time. If the note was meant to be prescriptive, then we have even more of a mystery on our hands. What was so wrong with the word? Why should Tocqueville or the Académie française want to banish it from serious discourse?

Paperwork was hard to take seriously. Most of Tocqueville's interlocutors remained unwilling to raise the topic at all. Guizot provided an excellent example of this reluctance in his treatise *The Means of Government and Opposition in the Current State of France*. "What are you doing then, you who proclaim that power is nothing but a hired servant who must be treated cheaply, whose activity and salary must be reduced as far as possible?" he demanded. "Do you not see that you completely misunderstand the dignity of power's nature and its relations with the people? A fine homage you render to the nation when you tell it that it obeys subordinates, that it receives its laws from clerks!" Of course, Guizot acknowledged, it sometimes did happen that clerks had more power that they ought to have. But the essence and interest of power lay elsewhere, "in chambers, public debate, elections, a free press, the jury."[55] It was as if power was somehow degraded through its association with paperwork; true power took the form of ideal speech situations. This phonocentric tendency in liberal and even radical political theory remains dominant to this day.

The fact that Tocqueville spent much of his career working with paperwork in one form or another is not a sufficient explanation for why he finally decided to write about it: many of the era's great liberals also worked for the state in various capacities. Nevertheless, Tocqueville's biography must have at least made him think. The son of a prefect, he began his own career as an apprentice judge in Versailles, adjudicating, among other cases, lawsuits involving lost titles and privileges from the Old Regime.[56] When he left for America in 1831, on a trip sponsored by the Ministry of the Interior, he must have been at least mildly curious to see how paperwork worked elsewhere. To his surprise, what he discovered was that there was hardly any paperwork at all.

Indeed, the missing paperwork constitutes an ongoing mystery throughout *Democracy in America*. "It is no good looking in the United States for uniformity and permanence of outlook, minute care of details, or perfection of administrative procedures," Tocqueville writes in one of the early chapters. "What one does find is a picture of power, somewhat wild perhaps, but robust, and a life liable to mishaps but full of striving and animation."[57] He elaborated on this theme in somewhat more detail in a later chapter, "Administrative Instability in the United States": "After one brief moment of power, officials are lost again amid the ever-changing crowd, and as a result, the proceedings of American society often leave fewer traces than do events in a private family. There is a sense in which public administration is oral and traditional. Nothing is written, or if it is, the slightest gust of wind carries it off, like Sibylline leaves, to vanish without recall." The allusion to the Sibyls was somewhat misplaced, perhaps, since the administrative documents under consideration recorded the past, rather than the future, but it nevertheless served to communicate what Tocqueville perceived as the otherworldly, ephemeral qualities of an administration based on oral tradition, rather than written documents. "I have no doubt that in fifty years' time it will be harder to collect authentic documents about the details of social life in modern America than about French medieval administration; and if some barbarian invasion caught the United States by surprise, in order to find out anything about the people who lived there one would have to turn to the history of other nations."[58]

Nor was it only hypothetical historians who suffered from the shortage of records. Real citizens were also in danger: "Nobody bothers about what was done before his time. No method is adopted; no archives are formed; no documents are brought together, even when it would be easy to do so. When by chance someone has them, he is casual about preserving them." Thus, several of his informants had simply handed over original documents to him, a practice that would surely not have been tolerated in the Archives nationales. This recklessness came at the expense of "the science of administration." "All sciences, to make progress, need to link the discoveries of succeeding generations," Tocqueville writes. "As life goes on, humanity collects various fruits of individual experience and builds up knowledge. It is very difficult for American administrators to learn anything from each other." Cognizant, perhaps, of Rousseau's aversion to paperwork, Tocqueville associates its absence with "democracy pressed to its ultimate limits." It "harms the art of government," he argues, and "is better adapted to a people whose administrative education is already finished than to a nation which is a novice in the experience of public affairs."[59]

Tocqueville's concern turned to outright alarm after he visited the Treasury Department and discovered that it was impossible to gather statistics on national resources and wealth, because the records did not exist. Granted, it would have been difficult to arrive at such numbers in France, as well, he wrote, but

> in America the idea of attempting that has not even been conceived. How can one hope to succeed in this new country where society has not yet taken settled and definite shape, where the national government has not at its disposal, as ours has, a crowd of agents whose efforts can be commanded and directed simultaneously, and finally, where the art of statistics is not cultivated, since no one has the chance of collecting documents or time to go through them?[60]

As for taxes, the federal and state governments published an exact accounting of their revenues, but those of the towns and counties were anyone's guess. "If the state wanted to obtain the information we need, it would encounter great obstacles from the negligence of inferior officials whose services it would have to use. Moreover, it is useless to inquire what the Americans might do in such a matter, for it is certain that up till now they have done nothing."[61]

In effect, the trip to America allowed Tocqueville to make a distinction between paperwork as such and the culture of paperwork that surrounded it. The former was an instrument of accountability; the latter an opportunity for impunity. He could have been talking about Balzac's protagonist Rabourdin when he wrote, in the second book of *Democracy in America*, about how "in the United States, when a citizen has some education and some resources he tries to enrich himself either by trade and industry or by buying a field covered in forest and turning into a pioneer." The situation was quite different in Europe. "As soon as a man begins to feel his strength and extend his ambitions, the first idea that occurs to him is to get an official appointment." Tocqueville was firm in his condemnation of this career path: "There is no need for me to say that this universal and uncontrolled desire for official appointments is a great social evil, that it undermines every citizen's sense of independence and spreads a venal and servile temper throughout the nation, that it stifles manly virtues."[62]

Not coincidentally, it was around the time that he was writing these words that Tocqueville began his own career in public administration. He was elected to Chamber of Deputies in 1839 to represent the circumscription of Valognes, in Normandy. Three years later, he was also elected to the Conseil Général de la Manche. The *conseils généraux* were the descendants of the departmental assemblies established by the Constituent Assembly in 1789; they had been abolished in the Year II by the Committee of Public Safety, only to be reestablished in the Year VIII by Napoleon and then reorganized in 1838 by the July Monarchy. They were responsible, in coordination with the prefects, for the execution of a wide variety of administrative tasks, from levying taxes and drawing up departmental budgets to managing public buildings, handling the pension funds of prefectoral employees, and providing for abandoned children.[63]

Tocqueville devoted tremendous time and energy to his administrative responsibilities; his biographer recounts that he often felt overwhelmed by the work of the Conseil Général.[64] The council divided its labors into various commissions; Tocqueville started out in the Commission d'Administration Générale, laboriously gathering prefectoral *arrêtés* and ministerial *circulaires* into dossiers for reports on various subjects. His most ambitious report concerned the construction of a railway line between Paris and Cherbourg. In letter after letter, he requested documents, complained of the difficulties in obtaining them, and apologized for the resulting delays in drawing up the report itself. Tocqueville finally completed an submitted the report to the minister of the interior in November 1844. Directly afterward he wrote a letter to the prefect apologizing for not sending him a copy, as well: "This document was too voluminous for me to be able to send it to you without spending a large amount on the post."[65]

His experience as an administrator may well have forced

Tocqueville to reevaluate his earlier arguments about centralization. In the notes to *Democracy in America* and then again in his important essay "On The Social and Political Condition of France Before and After 1789" that he published in John Stuart Mill's *London and Westminster Review*, Tocqueville had emphasized the essential continuities between prerevolutionary and postrevolutionary administration. By 1846, however, he had abandoned this thesis. In a report to the Académie des Sciences Morales et Politiques, for example, Tocqueville argued that "The French Revolution, which introduced so many novelties in the world, created nothing that was as new at the part of political law relating to the administration. Here, nothing resembles what preceded it; almost everything is of a recent date: the functions as well as the functionaries, the obligations as well as the guarantees." Far from providing evidence of continuity, the administration revealed a radical break in French history. "Not only does the French administration of our day not resemble the one that existed in the Old Regime, it is also profoundly different from the administrations of the principal contemporary nations. In this respect, one could say that our administrative institutions have a much more original character than our political institutions."[66]

The subject of this report was a treatise by the eminent jurist Louis-Antoine Macarel, who had worked his way up from a clerk in the postal administration in 1814, to a lawyer in the Conseil du Roi and the Cour de Cassation in 1822, to a member of the Conseil d'État in 1830, and then to Directeur de l'administration centrale et communale in the Ministry of the Interior in 1837; it was in this last capacity that he was charged with the 1838 reform of the departmental councils on which Tocqueville served. The two men had also participated together in a royal commission on Algeria for the Ministry of War.[67] Praising Macarel's *Cours de droit administrative* for its insights into the intricacies of the French administration, Tocqueville writes that it "takes us step by step down the immense ladder on which are placed one on top of another, without confusion but almost without end, the multitude of functionaries who compose among us the administrative hierarchy, from the king to the least agent of authority." In addition to providing a synchronic description of each administrative function, Macarel offered a diachronic account of its emergence. Tocqueville especially appreciated this historical element, which proved that there had been a rupture during the first years of the French Revolution. "Napoleon innovated much less in administration that is assumed and repeated.—Almost all of our administrative organization is the work of the Constituent Assembly: It laid down all the principles on which the administrative organization still rests; its hand formed, delimited, and armed almost all of the powers composing our administration, and then placed them in the positions they occupy relative to each other."[68]

We find none of the alarm that we have come to expect from Tocqueville. In this report, at least, he expresses enthusiasm for the nation's historical path. "Only in France was there a revolution so radical and so complete that they could reconstruct everything at the same time in the same place," he tells his readers. "One would truly have to be a friend of confusion and diversity not to build a new edifice in a regular manner."[69] At the same time, he reminded readers that they must "never lose from your sight that if our system of administration was conceived by liberty, it was completed by despotism: How to reconcile the extreme centralization that it consecrates with the reality and morality of representative government?" Further investigation would be necessary. "This book, messieurs, would be, in my opinion, one of the greatest works to which our generation could devote itself."[70]

Ten tough years later, this book was done. Hayden White has singled out *The Old Regime and the Revolution* as one of the most outstanding examples of the Tragic view of history. "Like his great contemporary, the novelist Balzac, Tocqueville exulted in the mystery of the fact that man 'has' a history," White writes. "But his conception of the dark abysses out of which man arises, and against which he throws up 'society' as a barrier to total chaos, did not permit him to hope for anything other than modest gains, from time to time, in his knowledge of the forces that ultimately govern the world process."[71] François Furet and Françoise Mélonio arrive at a similar interpretation. The book is "a modern tragedy in which the hero was overwhelmed not by Providence or by the laws of history but by his own consent to servitude and his unconscious desire for a master."[72]

Yet the tragic plot has a comic twist. We could read any number of the chapters of *The Old Regime and the Revolution* for style, insight, and intelligence. But there is only one chapter that might be read for a laugh. And it is no coincidence that this is the same chapter where Tocqueville had to remind himself to avoid referring to "bureaucracy." As in the examples mentioned earlier, this comic effect is achieved when the "spiritual purity of tragedy" is interrupted by the "eruption of materiality." And as in the earlier examples, this is not just any materiality, but the materiality of paperwork.

The chapter, "Administrative Moeurs under the Old Regime," is placed almost halfway through Tocqueville's book, as if it were a sort of entr'acte. The chapter's title may well have been an allusion to Ymbert's *Moeurs administratives* or to another satire strongly influenced by Ymbert, Boucher de Perthes's *Petit glossaire, traduction de quelques mots financiers, esquisses de moeurs administratives* (1835). But even if Tocqueville was unaware of these texts, the chapter stands out from the rest of the book and indeed from the rest of his work in its resonance with popular forms. The chapter opens with a challenge that could have been taken verbatim from Ymbert. "There is no way," he writes, "that one could read the correspondence of an intendant of the Old Regime with his superiors and subordinates without admiring how the resemblance between institutions renders the administrators of that era just like those of our time."[73] Even in the Old Regime, Tocqueville continues, "the minister had already conceived the desire to see every detail of every affair with his own eyes and to resolve everything himself from Paris." Crucially, this was not an idea—like Bentham's Panopticon, with which Tocqueville was familiar from his research into prisons—but a "desire" and a "passion." This "désir de pénétrer avec ses propre yeux" (literally, "to penetrate with his own eyes") was as much about the minister's voyeuristic impulses as about state surveillance. "The mass of writings was already enormous," Tocqueville tells us. So were the delays: even the simplest requests could take one, two, three years while local authorities waited for permission from Paris. He cites a 1773 edict of the Royal Council in which this absurdity was not only recognized, but consecrated: "Administrative formalities are leading to infinite delays in business and too often provoking complaints that are fully justified; nevertheless these formalities are absolutely necessary."[74] How was it possible for both the complaints and the objects of those complaints to be legitimate?

The administration of the Old Regime was ahead of its time in other ways. By the 1780s, the controller-general was sending out preprinted forms—"petits formes tout imprimés," little forms with printing all over them—to *intendants*, subdelegates, and other local sources in search of information. What he got back, Tocqueville quips, "was neither less detailed nor more accurate than what our subprefects and mayors provide today in the same circumstances.... Even the administrative languages of the two eras bear a striking resemblance. In both, the style is equally colorless, smooth, vague, and mushy. The physiognomy of each writer is effaced, lost in the common mediocrity. Who reads a prefect reads an *intendant*."[75]

As the chapter continues, Tocqueville shares some of the more exasperating exchanges he had found in the archives. A minister sends out requests to the *intendants* for news to fill the *Gazette de France* and hears back about the birth of triplets and a storm that caused no damage. Rules and regulations replaced one another so quickly that compliance became impossible. Those that weren't reversed by the state were inevitably modified in practice. Rather than encouraging independence, as it had the United States, this administrative instability left the French increasingly dependent on their government for resources, recognition, and other objects. The proudest gentlemen and the meekest peasants filled the in-boxes of Paris with requests for handouts. "The cartons that contain these," Tocqueville writes, "are perhaps the only places where all of the classes that made up the society of the Old Regime mingled."[76] With the chapter's conclusion, we also come to the end of this lighter tone. The next chapter, "How France Was Already, of All the Countries in Europe, the One Whose Capital Had Acquired the Greatest Predominance Over the Provinces and Best Absorbed the Entire Empire," opens with a sentence as ponderous as its title: "It is neither the location, nor the grandeur, nor the wealth of capitals that is the cause of their political predominance over the rest of the empire, but the nature of their government."[77] In other words, it's back to work for the reader. Good work, to be sure, but work, all the same.

A Bitter Joke

"Our literature sets the tone for all other literatures; the fashions of our elegant women are hastily adopted by elegant women of both the Old and New World. And then there is the bureaucracy!" Was there, asked Pierre Larousse in his *Grand dictionnaire universel du XIXe siècle*, "a country that can, not contest our preeminence, which is well established, but even claim to trail far behind us on this terrain?" What made France's bureaucracy so spectacular was its passion for accountability. "Proudhon says somewhere that double-entry bookkeeping, the science of owed and owned, with accounts that keep track of one another, is one of the masterpieces of the human spirit. But our bureaucracy must be even more admirable, because everything that takes place there is not only audited one time, but this audit is audited, and then the audit of the audit is audited." He recalled how "Madame de Sévigné claims to have known an old woman who could say 'My daughter, go tell your daughter's daughter that her daughter's daughter is crying.' So it is with the story of the audit of the audit that is itself audited."[78]

He was joking, Larousse told his readers, but only sort of. "There is bitterness in our joke, because this mania for scribbling and subjecting even the most simple acts to needlessly complicated formalities and paperwork is one of the biggest obstacles to the introduction of the most desirable reforms in our country." France was overwhelmed by "enormous registers, covered with words and numbers added with great trouble, never again to be read or consulted by anyone"; it had been submerged in "loose sheets of paper, representing the daily labor of a multitude of copyists, passing through the hands of a crowd of higher employees who sign without reading them." Thwarting political reforms, obstructing social progress, the bureaucracy now constituted "a state within the state, truly a power to be reckoned with."[79]

In book 11, chapter 6 of *The Spirit of the Laws*, Montesquieu famously distinguished between three kinds of state power:

> legislative power, executive power over the things depending on the right of nations, and executive power over the things depending on civil right.—By the first, the prince or the magistrate makes laws for a time or for always and corrects or abrogates those that have been made. By the second, he makes peace or war, sends or receives embassies, establishes security, and prevents invasions. By the third, he punishes crimes or judges disputes between individuals. The last will be called the power of judging, and the former simply the executive power of the state.[80]

Here we have one of the foundational distinctions of modern political thought in its theoretical and especially in its applied modes. But this separation of powers also separates power as such from the realities of the modern state. This was the point of Gournay's little joke when he coined the term "bureaucracy."

With Tocqueville, paperwork enters into "serious" political theory. But the condition of its entry, the special stamp on its entry permit, requires that theorists not take it too seriously. The slippage in genre—from Montesquieu to Balzac and back again—reflects how hard it is for political theory to conceive of paperwork in its material and psychic reality. From a psycho-analytic perspective, this is in part because paperwork's symbolic function—its function of telling us about the world and what to do or what not to do to it—keeps collapsing back into its imaginary dimension: the dimension of attachment and aggression. The minister does not just need to know, he wants to know; and he does not just want to know, he wants to see; and he does not just want to see, he wants to penetrate us with his eyes. And the citizen does not just need help, he wants help; and he does not just want help, he wants to feel something. In a world of rights, he wants to feel privileged.

Modern political theory will have to turn and return to fiction in its efforts to grasp this split reality. "Since the nineteenth century," Foucault tells us,

> an essential feature of big Western bureaucracies has been that the administrative machine, with its unavoidable effects of power, works by using the mediocre, useless, imbecilic, superficial, ridiculous, worn-out, poor, and powerless functionary. The administrative grotesque has not been merely that kind of visionary perception of administration that we find in Balzac, Dostoevsky, Courteline, or Kafka. The administrative grotesque is a real possibility for bureaucracy. Ubu the "pen pusher" is a functional component of modern administration, just as being in the hands of a mad charlatan was a function of Roman imperial power.[81]

He might just as easily have summoned up Gogol, Dickens, Conrad, Heller, Saramago, or Terry Gilliam. It's not only citizens or the state that are wanting; political theory is also wanting. Fiction will keep filling, but never quite fill, that lack.

CHAPTER FOUR

The Bureaucratic Medium

"It was a revolution beside which the French Revolution was child's play, a world struggle beside which the struggles of the Diadochi appear insignificant. Principles ousted one another, heroes of the mind overthrew each other with unheard-of rapidity, and in the three years 1842–45 more of the past was swept away in Germany than at other time in three centuries. All this is supposed to have taken place in the realm of pure thought."[1] Thus Karl Marx reflected back on his first years out of university. He received his degree from the law faculty at Berlin in spring 1841. Like many of his friends (and many of ours), he had little or no hope of finding academic employment, so he moved back in with his parents, making occasional trips to Trier, Bonn, and Cologne.[2] Following an especially nasty argument with his mother in the summer 1842, he moved out of the house and into the world. His family refused to support him any further, so he turned first to freelance journalism and then to full-time employment as the editor of a local newspaper, the *Rheinische Zeitung*, which was backed by a local group of liberal industrialists. Over the next year, Marx would build a reputation as an editor and critic without equal. Circulation took off; censors took notice. "Imagine Rousseau, Voltaire, Holbach, Lessing, Heine, and Hegel fused into one person," an acquaintance wrote of the editor, then only twenty-four years old. "I say fused not juxtaposed—and you have Dr. Marx."[3] He made this reputation not only through media, but with media as a privileged object of practical-theoretical reflection. This moment in his career has been almost entirely neglected by the sorts of scholars we might expect to be interested in these sorts of things. Marx as media theorist?

The last decade or so has seen what we might call a "technical turn" in the humanities. Inspired largely by science studies, humanists have started to think seriously about the technics of knowledge. With respect to the history and theory of paperwork, we can probably trace this approach back to Bruno Latour's essay "Visualization and Cognition: Drawing Things Together," which illustrated how science studies might illuminate the production of other kinds of official or quasi-official knowledge. "The 'rationalization' granted to bureaucracy since Hegel and Weber has been attributed by mistake to the 'mind' of (Prussian) bureaucrats," Latour argues. "It is all in the files themselves. A bureau is, in many ways, and more and more every year, a small laboratory in which many elements can be connected together just because their scale and nature has been averaged out: legal texts, specifications, standards, payrolls, maps, surveys."[4] Latour's call for an "ethnography of inscription" has fulfilled its intellectual promise time and again, not least in Latour's own study of jurisprudenc. Through subtle reconstructions of knowledge infrastructures and actor networks, the ethnographer is able to reconstruct the law's specific mode of truth production in all of its wondrous tedium.

Latour's work is by no means the only version of antihermeneutics to find an audience among former critical theorists. These days we must also contend with affect theory, several varieties of surface reading, and those multitudinous vitalisms, not to mention models of interpretation that claim to be based on evolutionary psychology, cognitive science, and computer science. That the foremost spokesman for the venerable Freudo-Marxist project tends toward an antic Hegelianism—first time as tragedy, second time as farce—has not helped matters much.

The case of paperwork will not settle the controversy over the hermeneutics of suspicion, but it might unsettle it. Throughout this book, I have argued that paperwork is unpredictable. I have attributed this unpredictability to the fact that paperwork is first and foremost a medium of communication, particularly written communication, and thus subject to the material and semiotic exigencies of *différance*. To put this argument a bit more crudely, shit happens. However, as anyone who has ever raised a child or read a novel by Philip Roth knows, shit doesn't *only* "happen." It can also be part of a struggle in which pleasure and unpleasure, love and aggression, conscious and unconscious motivation all play a role. In paperwork, as in potty training, some accidents are less accidental than others.

No matter how tired we are of the hermeneutics of suspicion—and it can certainly get tiresome—we must not forget that sometimes our suspicions have turned out to be correct. In Florida during the 2000 presidential election, the dimpled chads were purely and simply accidental: the perforation machine had not been correctly calibrated for that year's card stock. The flaws in the butterfly ballot, on the other hand, were the product of a different kind of error—not deliberate, to be sure, but not exactly accidental, either. This chapter turns to Marx and Freud in an attempt to outline a theory of paperwork's powers and failures that recognizes the possibility of such overdetermination. Not only does paperwork require a theory of *praxis*, a theory that takes its materiality as a point of departure, it also requires a theory of *parapraxis*, a theory that recognizes that paperwork, like any form of communication, is subject to unconscious forces. Their lessons emerge in unexpected places: a short article about a tax dispute involving Mosel winemakers, an even briefer account of a trip to the Austrian Postal Savings Bank to withdraw money for a sick relative. But where else would we expect to find paperwork? I will conclude the chapter by taking us to back to France, where Roland Barthes has been waiting for us, patiently, all along.

The Case of Inspector von Zuccalmaglio

We can imagine Marx felt proud when, in 1842, he published his first article in the *Rheinische Zeitung*. He had certainly worked hard on it. The target was a set of new rules on press censorship that had been favorably covered in the *Preussische Staats-Zeitung*, a quasi-governmental newspaper—or in Marx's wickedly insulting phrase, its "semi-official press-child."[5] The editors of the *Staats-Zeitung* had tried to justify the merits of the latest rules on the censorship of newspapers by reminding readers of the many print formats that were not subject to these rules, particularly certain kinds of academic publication. Marx seized on the evident discomfort of the newspaper in reporting on censorship to make his case for full freedom of the press.

The article is worth lingering over for a moment if only because it reveals a young man attuned to the era's "bibliographic imagination."[6] "Our time has no longer that real taste for size that we admire in the Middle Ages," Marx tells his readers.

> Look at our paltry little pietistic tracts, look at our philosophical systems in small octavo, and then cast your eyes on the twenty gigantic folios of Duns Scotus. You do not need to read the books; their exciting aspect suffices to touch your heart and strike your senses, something like a Gothic cathedral. These primitive gigantic works materially affect the mind; it feels oppressed under their mass, and the feeling of oppression is the beginning of awe. You do not master books, they master you.[7]

This is not Marx's voice, exactly, but a parody of the editors of the *Staats-Zeitung* as they tried to rest their case in favor of press censorship on a distinction between print formats, that is to say, on the basis of size, rather than content. "The child holds the big man to be a great man, and in the same childish way the *Staats-Zeitung* informs us that thick books are incomparably better than thin ones, and much more so than single leaflets or newspapers, which produce only one printed sheet daily."[8]

For Marx, such an attitude was typical of what he called a "childish-sensuous" materialism, that is, a materialism based on objects rather than processes. Such a materialism "tells us that in regard to railways one should only think of rails and ways, in regard to trade contracts only of sugar and coffee, and in regard to leather factories only of leather." This theory "does not go beyond sensuous perception, it sees a thing only in isolation, and the invisible nerve threads which link the particular with the universal, which in the state as everywhere make the material parts into soul-possessing members of the spiritual whole, are for the child non-existent."[9] Wai Chee Dimock has pointed to Marx's habitual reliance on the logic of metonymy to establish causation, a habit that does not always serve the logic of his argument especially well; here we catch him trying to conceal these logical problems behind the vaguely paranoid metaphor of the "invisible nerve threads" linking the part to the whole.[10] Yet Marx was on a deadline, and under the circumstances, he didn't do so badly. We can see him developing what would soon become his critique of Feuerbach and the Young Hegelians; significantly, this critique began as an attack on the object-oriented materialism afflicting the history and theory of media.[11]

This article appeared in May 1842. The following October, Marx published his next major exposé, a report on debates over the law against the theft of wood, a critical question with winter coming. And then, in January 1843, he published what would be his last article for the *Rheinische Zeitung*, since the authorities abolished the newspaper immediately thereafter. This article, I would argue, is the most radical and articulate theory of media in Marx's oeuvre. Entitled "Justification of the Correspondent from the Mosel," it was a response to a rescript from the provincial *Oberpräsident* demanding evidence of several claims made about his administration by the newspaper. The *Oberpräsident* was especially unhappy about a claim in an article concerning a tax dispute between the Prussian administration and the winemakers of the Mosel region. The author of that article, a local lawyer, had argued that "the cry of distress of the vine-growers was for a long time regarded in higher quarters as an insolent shrieking." The *Oberpräsident* wrote that "I think I can in advance certainly describe this assertion as untrue."[12]

The occasion for the original article had been a steep drop in the price of wine. The Society for the Promotion of Viticulture in the Mosel-Saar and Trier had petitioned the Ministry of Finance for tax breaks to help its members through this difficult period. The government in Trier had then dispatched the chief of the Trier Cadastre Bureau, a tax inspector named von Zuccalmaglio, to check the numbers reported by the winemakers in support of their petition. Von Zuccalmaglio was well suited to this task since, several years earlier, he had cooperated with the Society for the Promotion of Viticulture to compile the registers that served as the basis for the industry's most recent decennial statistical report. Inspector von Zuccalmaglio dutifully visited the winemakers, listened to their problems, examined the vineyards, and reviewed what new numbers he could find. He then returned to Trier and filed a report concluding that there was no basis for a tax reduction. The authorities deliberated over the report for several months before reaching a decision: "The state will be able to confine itself solely to making the transition as easy as possible for the present population by appropriate measures."[13]

No wonder the winemakers were upset. But could the state really be accused of regarding these cries of distress as "insolent shrieking"? When Marx and the other editors asked the correspondent who had written the article to provide evidence to back up this claim, he came up short, so Marx took it upon himself to write the response. Yes the *Oberpräsident* and other authorities had regarded these cries of distress in precisely this way; they could not have done otherwise. Their reaction was not a reflection of carelessness or callousness, but a specific effect of the material and psychic realities of what Marx named "the bureaucratic medium." The conflict had to be understood as the result of a specific conjuncture precipitated by the state's reliance on paperwork.

The article on the Mosel situation takes the form of a thought experiment. Let's assume that there is the rule of law, even if we don't like this or that particular law; let's assume, too, that everyone operates with the best of intentions, even if we don't particularly like them. Why does the state still stumble when it intervenes in local affairs? Marx approached this problem through the juxtaposition of the petition of the Society for the Promotion of Viticulture and the report of the chief of the Cadastre Bureau. It's all very technical: the yield per *morgen*; the price of a *fuder* sold in the autumn; how to calculate the cost of the barrel; the wisdom of removing lateral shoots from the grapevines, which increases the quality of the wine, but decreases its quantity. As we move back and forth between excerpts from the tax inspector's report and from the trade group's responses to each of his points, we become aware of an incommensurability between the two discourses. Paradoxically, the incommensurability emerges precisely at that point of apparent commensurability, that is to say, in the exchange of documents.

Marx asks us to consider Inspector von Zuccalmaglio's position. He has been chosen because of his expertise in the wine industry and his familiarity with the Mosel region. How could he not feel a bit defensive when he reads the complaints about his work?

> He is aware of his conscientious performance of his duty and of the detailed official information at his disposal; he is suddenly faced with an opposing view, and what could be more natural than that he should take sides against the petitioner, and that the intentions of the latter, which could of course always be bound up with private interests, should seem to him suspicious, and that therefore he should suspect them.[14]

Von Zuccal maglio's suspicions are raised that much further by the fact that the accusations come not from the majority of the winemakers, but from a few troublemakers among them, the kind who take part in something like a Society for the Promotion of Viticulture. "The obviously poor vine-grower has neither the time nor the education to describe his condition; hence the poor vine-grower is unable to speak, whereas the vine cultivator who is able to speak is not obviously poor, and therefore his complaints seem unfounded."[15]

Naturally, the winemakers are also upset. If the officials only knew the truth, they would understand the urgency of assisting them. Thus the producers "cannot avoid suspecting that behind total misconception of their account of the actual state of affairs, which is based on well-founded convictions and clear facts, there is a selfish intention, namely, the intention to assert official judgment in opposition to the intelligence of the citizens." The officials respond that on the contrary, they have already sent one of their most experienced inspectors, who in turn has filed a report that shows, more or less clearly, that there is nothing to be done right now. The rules are the rules. "Whether the administrative principles and institutions are good or not is a question that lies outside his sphere, for that can only be judged in higher quarters where a wider and deeper knowledge of the official nature of things, i.e., of their connection with the state as a whole, prevails."[16]

We seem to be witnessing a reenactment of the lord-and-bondsman scene from Hegel's *Phenomenology*. But we should also notice the differences. The participants are feeling self-conscious, to be sure, but not in the Hegelian mode. Their self-consciousness arises from a feeling of derealization, rather than depersonalization; that is to say, the split is experienced as an aspect of reality, instead of an aspect of the self. The winemakers look at the world around them, study the official report on the world around them, and begin to get that uncanny feeling. The world as they know it seems to be threatened by a virtual world made up of notes, dossiers, reports. "The most patent reality appears illusory when compared with the reality depicted in the dossiers," Marx writes, "which is official and therefore of a state character." The state "has once and for all established principles, it has its official picture of the region in the cadastre, it has official data on revenue and expenditure, it has everywhere, alongside the actual reality, a bureaucratic reality, which retains authority however much times may change."[17] The more the winemakers point to this split in reality, the crazier they seem to the officials, who might feel sorry for them, who might even think they understand how they feel, but who are also convinced that they have already done everything in their power to help. Whether the officials should have more power is not for them to decide. Besides, the state can't give in to a demand simply because the subject of the demand feels strongly about it. That really would be crazy.

Thus, the two parties arrive at an impasse. The winemakers, by trying to voice their distress, have come to seem either crazy or selfish; the officials, by trying to perform their duty, now seem callous or corrupt. What could be done to resolve this impasse? Only another form of mediation, one that would be capable of repairing the split between material and psychic realities. "The rulers and the ruled alike are in need of a third element which would be political without being official, hence not based on bureaucratic premises, an element which would be of a civil nature without being bound up with private interests and their pressing need."[18]

This "third element" was a free press. Unlike paperwork, with its rational formats and protocols, the free press could speak both the language of reason and the language of sentiment. "The attitude of the press to the people's conditions of life is based on reason, but it is equally based on feeling. Hence it does not speak only in the clever language of judgment that soars above circumstances, but the passionate language of circumstances themselves, a language which cannot and should not be demanded of official reports." Only a free press, that is, would be capable of expressing "the people's need in its real shape, not refracted through any bureaucratic medium."[19]

This conception of paperwork as a medium through which need is refracted suggests two tentative conclusions. First, paperwork is a refractive medium in that power and knowledge inevitably change their speed and shape when they enter it. Inevitably, but not invariably—it is precisely this variability that makes paperwork so tricky. Not only does it accelerate and decelerate power, it syncopates its rhythms, disrupts its cycles, which is why paperwork always seems to be either overdue or underdone. And second, paperwork is a refractory medium in that it is inevitably (but again, not invariably) uncooperative and unpredictable. Pierre Marc de Biasi has characterized paper as the "fragile support of the essential," but we might do better to think of it as the essential support of the fragile: letters and numbers, but also needs and wants.[20] The winemakers of the Mosel valley need and want something not only from Inspector von Zuccalmaglio, but from Inspector von Zuccalmaglio 's report: resources, recognition, and something else that remains elusive, perhaps even to them. This extra something is what Marx believes the press will reflect, rather than refract; we can see him straining against the limits of contemporary psychology in his search to name it. And it is this extra something that means, for Marx, that we must always be suspicious of paperwork—not of each others' motives, but of the medium as such. It never rests, so never should we. Thus Marx constitutes paperwork as a proper object of theoretical praxis.

Smashing

If critical theorists have remained unaware of this article, it can only be because of our own difficulty in taking paperwork seriously. As we saw in Tocqueville, the reference to "bureaucracy" is a symptom of this difficulty. It would be difficult for Marx, too, and for the Marxist theory of the state throughout the era of the Second and Third Internationals. In the months and years following the defense of the Mosel winemakers, Marx returned several times to the problems of what, using an old metaphor, he called the "machinery" of the state.[21] But the presumption of good faith that makes the article on the Mosel region so subtle—so attentive to both material and psychic reality—is abandoned for a form of paranoid criticism much closer to what he had found among the winemakers themselves. The more he observed it at work, the more he thought about it, the more he abandoned the idea that this machine could be tinkered with, repaired, or improved in any significant way. The only remaining option, as we know, would be to smash it and start all over again.

The *Rheinische Zeitung* was suppressed before Marx was able to publish all of the installments of his article on the Mosel controversy (including one section entitled, enticingly, "The Vampires of the Mosel Region"). Freed of his journalistic duties, Marx returned to philosophy proper. The earliest of his major critical endeavors is the uncompleted manuscript from the summer of 1843, the "Critique of Hegel's Philosophy of Right (§261–313)," which provides a detailed commentary on central passages of Hegel's major work of political philosophy. The premise of Marx's critique is that Hegel had given the Prussian state "the stamp of philosophical approval." Nowhere was this collusion more apparent, Marx believed, than in Hegel's passages on administration, which "could be inserted word for word as they stand in the Prussian Legal Code."[22] Marx was especially indignant about Hegel's famous elevation of functionaries such as Inspector von Zuccalmaglio to the status of the "universal estate" or "class," that is, the only class with "the universal interests of society as its business."[23]

Where Hegel spoke of administration (*die Verwaltung, die Regierung*), Marx counters with references to "bureaucracy." "Bureaucracy is the imaginary state alongside the real state," he writes. "It is the spiritualism of the state. Hence everything acquires a double meaning: a real meaning and a bureaucratic one; in like fashion, there is both real knowledge and bureaucratic knowledge (and the same applies to the will)." When Marx does allude to the materiality of this institution, it is a vulgar materialism of personal interest, rather than the more nuanced materialism of the Mosel article. "This spiritualism degenerates into crass materialism, the materialism of passive obedience, the worship of authority, the mechanism of fixed, formal action, of rigid principles, views, and traditions. As for the individual bureaucrat, the purpose of the state becomes his private purpose, a hunt for promotion, careerism," he continues. "The state thus exists only as a series of fixed bureaucratic minds held together by passive obedience and their subordinate position in a hierarchy." Marx returns several times to the figure of the Jesuit to stress this curious mixture of passivity and activity that character-izes the "bureaucratic mind": "Whether consciously or uncon-sciously the bureaucrat must behave Jesuitically towards the real state."[24]

This gesture toward the unconscious (*bewusstlos*) motivation is one of the only remaining traces of the subtle psychopathol-ogy of paperwork that he had sketched the previous year. Marx had adopted the language of Ymbert and Balzac. And indeed, a catalogue of his personal library from 1850 shows that he owned a copy of Ymbert's *Moeurs administratives*. (It is somewhat better known that he translated Peuchet's book on suicide and that he planned a study of Balzac.)[25] In an era when the word "bureau-cracy" was still rare in the German language—there is no men-tion of it the Grimm brothers' dictionary, though it makes an appearance in Rotteck and Welker's *Staatslexicon*—Marx employs it with abandon. The tone changes accordingly. What about Hegel's suggestion that civil servants be recruited through a system of examinations? "In a rational state it would be more appropriate to ensure that a cobbler passed an examination than an executive civil servant." Cobbling, after all, requires special-ized knowledge. This is a recognizably Rousseauean argument, to which Marx added an appropriately Rousseauean flourish: "It is not recorded that Greek and Roman statesman ever took examinations. But then what is a Roman statesman compared to a Prussian civil servant!"[26] What about Hegel's argument in favor of generous salaries for civil servants as a prophylactic against corruption? "In §294 Hegel derives the payment of salaries to officials from the Idea."[27]

As with Balzac or Tocqueville, the efflorescence of the rheto-ric of "bureaucracy" brings insights along with oversights. In early 1844, Marx officially transferred the title of "universal class" from the bureaucrats to the proletariat. He announced his discovery, which was made in Paris, in the *Deutsch-Französische Jahrbücher*. The proletariat is "a group which has a universal character because of its universal suffering and which lays claim to no particular right because the wrong it suffers is not a particular wrong but wrong in general." In place of the discredited alliance between Hegelian idealism and the Prussian state, there emerged a heroic alliance between materialist philosophy and the working class. "Philosophy cannot realize itself without the sublation of the proletariat, and the proletariat cannot sublate itself without the realization of philosophy."[28]

The French Revolution was premised on Sieyès's theoretical discovery that paperwork resembles other kinds of work. The communist revolution, by contrast, was premised on a rejection of this equation. Where, we might ask, are the clerks in Engels's *Condition of the Working Class in England*? Or in the *Communist Manifesto*, where Marx and Engels decry the immiseration of "the physician, the lawyer, the priest, the poet, the man of science," but make no mention of the hundreds of thousands of young men laboring in offices?[29] To be sure, Marx and Engels had plenty of reason to be wary of the state and its agents, who, consciously or unconsciously, served the powers of counterrevolution. Still, we should pause to reflect on the consequences of this theoretical, or perhaps pretheoretical, omission. Imagine, for a moment, that the critique of capitalism had never moved beyond the denunciation of banks (or worse still, bank clerks) to an understanding of the commodity form; imagine that the critique of imperialism had never moved beyond the denunciation of Europe's navies to an understanding of primitive accumulation. The story of Marxist state theory after 1843 is a story of missed opportunities. When, in *The Eighteenth Brumaire of Louis Bonaparte*, Marx concludes that the lesson of history is that the only option left is to smash the state—Engels, ever the botanist, hopes that it will wither away—he has found himself in the same theoretical impasse that he had once shown us how to escape.[30]

Mistakes Are Made

If Marx provides a theory of praxis for the bureaucratic medium, Freud supplies a theory of parapraxis, or at least the beginnings of one. Not every paperwork problem has the world-historical or even microhistorical pathos of the struggle between the Mosel winemakers and the Prussian authorities. Most problems take place on a more intimate scale: a name misspelled, a sum miscalculated, a date misrecorded. Such errors contribute to paperwork's refractiveness, its refractoriness—they are essential to it—but they also trouble us in smaller, subtler ways. And of course, we are just as likely to be the subjects of these mistakes as the objects. Marx's central insight was that we should begin by suspecting the medium itself, rather than the motives behind it. Freud's conclusion is that we should in fact suspect our motives, though not quite the motives Marx had in mind. Freud works at a much smaller scale than Marx—he studies the surface of the paper itself, scrutinizing its every letter and number and still more microscopic traces. And what he discovers on this surface—not beneath it, but right there on its surface—is the unconscious. Or rather, not *the* unconscious, which would be too impersonal, too abstract, but *your* unconscious.

Freud's *Psychopathology of Everyday Life*, first published in 1901, is one of the most entertaining of his books, and one of the most radical.[31] Freud finally came out and said what he had hesitated to say in the final chapter of *The Interpretation of Dreams*: unconscious forces are at work in all of us, all the time. We are governed by forces that are both within us and beyond us. Even routine activities such as remembering where we put our car keys are susceptible to the exigencies of the unconscious—love, anger, envy, guilt. Which means, of course, that our paperwork might be, too. Carl Schorske famously argued that *The Interpretation of Dreams* evaded the political realities of the 1890s through a series of unconscious maneuvers: Oedipus Filius, never Oedipus Rex.[32] We might also notice the number of anecdotes in *The Psychopathology of Everyday Life* that refer to "bureaucratic" problems of one sort or another without ever identifying them as such: a committee member who routinely misses meetings, a father who bungles the name of his new child at the Registrar of Births. And then there are the large number of errors that involve other examples of practical literacy: spilled ink pots, mislabeled envelopes, misread train schedules. And here, too, we see the beginnings of a theory that seems unaware of its theoretical import: a parapractical theory of paperwork. Paradoxically, the first person to recognize this aspect of Freud's work was also one of his fiercest critics, the philologist Sebastiano Timpanaro.

The Psychopathology of Everyday Life opens with a train trip along the Dalmatian coast that Freud had taken late in the summer of 1898. He had been travelling from Dubrovnik to Kotor Varoš in Bosnia and Herzogovina when he fell into conversation with a lawyer from Berlin named Freyhau about the sexual customs of the Bosnian Muslims. Freud was about to tell Freyhau a story he had heard from a fellow physician—the punch line was, "Herr, what can you do?"—when he cut himself short, fearing that he might offend the lawyer's sensibilities. He switched the topic to some of the art he had recently seen on his trip. Had Freyhau ever seen the frescoes of the cathedral in Orvieto by . . . it was right there, on the tip of his tongue. He could even visualize the painter's self-portrait. He thought of Boticelli, but that wasn't right. *Boltraffio?*

The name that Freud was unable to produce was Signorelli. He shared the accident with Wilhelm Fliess when he got back to Vienna: "At last I found out the name, Signorelli, and immediately knew, on my own, the first name, Luca—as proof that it had been only a repression and not a genuine forgetting." The letter continues at a breathless pace:

> It is clear why Botticelli had moved into the foreground; only *Signor* was repressed; the *Bo* in both substitute names is explained by the memory responsible for the repression; it concerned something that happened in *Bosnia* and began with the words "Herr, what can be

done about it?" I lost the name of Signorelli during a short trip to *Herzegovina*, which I made from Ragusa with a lawyer from Berlin with whom I got to talking about pictures. In the conversation, which aroused memories that evidently caused the repression, we talked about death and sexuality. The word *Trafio* is no doubt an echo of Trafoi, which I saw on the first trip! How can I make this credible to anyone?[33]

How indeed? Freud tried twice, first in a short paper "The Psychical Mechanism of Forgetfulness," which appeared in a neurological journal in December 1898, and then again in the first chapter of *The Psychopathology of Everyday Life*. "Signorelli" is the specimen slip of psychoanalysis, just as "Irma's Injection" is its specimen dream. The 1898 version, Michael Molnar has pointed out, is "the first detailed examination of unconscious processes ever to be published."[34] In both versions, Freud illustrates the episode with a diagram that resembles nothing so much as a train map, with rails, switches, junctions, missed and unexpected connections—an accident waiting to happen (figure 6).

The diagram is best read from top to bottom. At the top are the elements closest to consciousness: Signorelli, whose self-portrait, but not name he is able to summon up quite clearly, and Boticelli and Boltraffio, the names that actually come to Freud's mind. Beneath these names we find Bosnia and Herzogovina, which is simultaneously the destination of his trip, the topic of his conversation, and the site of an important condensation and a displacement. The "Herr" of Herzogovina condenses its Italian equivalent, the "Signor" of Signorelli, as well as the entire punch line of Freud's preempted joke: "Herr, what's a man supposed to do?" Suddenly overwhelmed, Herzogovina passes some of its responsibility over to Bosnia, which finds its newly important role echoed in the first syllables of Boticelli and Boltraffio.

As we move down the diagram, we approach the causes of this lexical train wreck. Freud's joke connects to more troubling thoughts about death and sexuality. The Tyrolian resort town of Trafoi also clearly has some sort of role to play, since, like

124

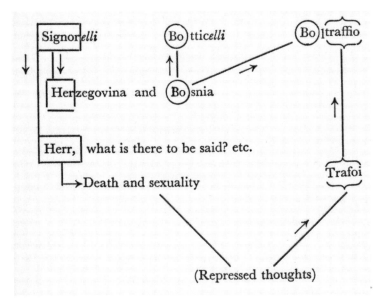

Figure 6. Freud's diagram of the "Signorelli" slip from *The Psychopathology of Everyday Life* (1901).

it ends up providing its phonemes to the folks up above. But the diagram does not stop there. There is something even deeper, something lurking at the very bottom of the diagram, concealed between parentheses: the repressed thoughts. Freud gave no hint of what those repressed thoughts were in either the letter to Fliess or the article of 1898. Only in *The Psychopathology of Everyday Life* do we get even a partial explanation. Freud had been visiting Trafoi when received news that "a patient over whom I had taken a great deal of trouble had put an end to his life on account of an incurable sexual disorder."[35] This forgetting was no mere accident. Nor was the substitution of the names Boticelli and Boltraffio for the forgotten name entirely random. Such slips, Freud concluded, "can be traced back to incompletely suppressed psychical material, which, although pushed away by consciousness, has nevertheless not been robbed of all capacity for expressing itself."[36]

Maurice Merleau-Ponty spoke for many when, responding to a lecture by Jacques Lacan in 1957, he commented that "I must admit that the Signorelli story that you have alluded to once again always troubles me. When one reads this text, as with many other psychoanalytic texts, if you're not one of the initiated, if you don't practice, if you haven't experienced it, you are always struck by how Freud always seems to want to turn things upside down rather than take them as they are." This Signorelli slip, he added, is a "fact of language [*langage*], a fact of speech [*parole*]."[37] Lacan came to Freud's defense, of course, but in subsequent lectures and essays used the example less and less frequently.[38] More recently, the Freud scholar Peter Swales has cast doubt not only on the theory behind the slip, but on some of the basic empirical claims in Freud's text, including whether he was even in Trafoi when he received the news of his patient's suicide.[39]

But the most powerful critique of Freud's theory of parapraxis was made by the philologist and philosopher Sebastiano Timpanaro. Born in Parma in 1923, he trained in Florence under Giorgio Pasquali, publishing a number of important and admired works of textual criticism—on Lucretius, Virgil, Ovid, Seneca, so forth—along with an influential study of the nineteenth-century classicist Karl Lachmann. A superb academic career, except that Timpanaro never held an academic position. He was an organic intellectual of white-collar odd-jobbers, paying his bills as a proofreader for a small publishing house. When he wasn't working or studying, he militated for a number of socialist and communist causes. In an obituary, historian Perry Anderson hailed him as "one of the purest and most original minds of the second half of the century."[40]

In 1974, Timpanaro published his critique of Freud's theory of parapraxis in a book entitled *The Freudian Slip: Psychoanalysis and Textual Criticism*. A chapter appeared in English in the *New Left Review* the following year, where it precipitated an intergenerational brawl in the British Left. Younger scholars such as Jacqueline Rose, Juliet Mitchell, and Peter Wollen published forceful responses criticizing Timpanaro's understanding of the basic principles of psychoanalysis.[41] But Timpanaro also had powerful supporters, among them an older group of British radicals. The psychoanalyst Charles Rycroft pronounced himself "in the main convinced by Timpanaro's demonstration that Freud's theory of slips does not hold water and reveals more about his social milieu than it does about psychological verities" (even if, in Rycroft's opinion, "Timpanaro has got contemporary psychoanalysis all wrong, and his conception of it bears little resemblance to the realities of its practice today in this country and the United States").[42] Still more enthusiastically, Raymond Williams wrote that Timpanaro had exposed "the arbitrary and tendentious character of certain Freudian interpretations," pointing the way toward a "fully materialist" theory of the slip.[43]

Put simply, Timpanaro's argument was that most of the errors offered by Freud as evidence of his theory were already familiar to "anyone who has practical experience with ancient texts, or of manuscripts or type-scripts or printer's proofs today."[44] They arise not from unconscious motives, but from the mechanical and cognitive challenges involved in producing and reproducing texts. You have to put yourself in the place of a scribe, compositor, typist, linotype operator, or phototypesetter whose hours are spent copying words and numbers from one sheet of paper to another or from sheet to compositor's stick, sheet to keyboard. There is a reason why a compositor has to mind his p's and q's rather than, say, his b's and d's: not only are they reverse images of one another—tricky when setting type from right to left—but they are also right next to each other in the tray (figure 7). A typist has to mind her q's and w's.

To these mechanical errors Timpanaro added cognitive ones. The most common of these is "banalization," when writers substitute more familiar words for less familiar ones. It is banalization, for example, when an undergraduate substitutes "fantasy echo" for "fin-de-siècle" in an in-class exam.[45] This is not only an auditory phenomenon, but a visual one. In alphabetic scripts, for example, words are recognized by their silhouettes—their "boumas"— as much as by the sequence of their letters.[46] It is thus easy,

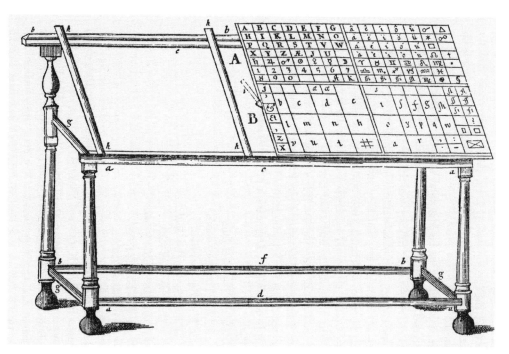

Figure 7. A type case from Joseph Moxon's *Mechanick Exercises; or The Doctrine of Handy-Works Applied to the Art of Printing* (1683).

especially when reading quickly, to mistake one word for another with a similar shape; in cases of bad handwriting, it is sometimes the only feature one can go by. We could speculate that there are unconscious motives behind this misrecognition, but why bother? It seems much more plausible that the student heard the word pronounced in lecture, skipped the chance to see it spelled out in the week's reading, and made his or her best guess.

Even when a word is recognized correctly, it can easily become confused with a more familiar word in the scribe's working memory. Unless the original material was in an unknown language or script, the scribe would work by memorizing shorter or longer sequences of words before recording them on the sheet of paper in front of him. The need to keep referring back to a text explains some larger errors, as well. The *saut du même au même* occurs when a copyist skips a word or line in the original text and takes it up again farther along. A similar mistake is dipthography, or the repetition of words, phrases, or lines that have already been copied. "It can very easily happen, even writing original texts rather than transcriptions, that we commit errors of repetition," Timpanaro explains, "because our thoughts and their transmission do not always proceed at the same rate, and the writer can have the mistaken impression that he still has to write down something that he in fact has already written."[47] Thus even "higher order" errors can be explained more easily by motor cognition than by unconscious forces.

The Signorelli incident is an example of banalization. Like "fantasy echo," "Boticelli" represented the more familiar of two phonically similar words. Drawing on his considerable erudition, Timpanaro provided examples of banalization from Cicero and Macrobius, Tasso and Heine, even from Mussolini, who, shortly before Allied forces landed in Sicily, opened a speech with a reflection on how "The Greek philosopher Anaxagoras (forgive my erudition) said that man is the measure of all things." He meant to say Protagoras. Even in a case like this, where the substitution arose from a kind of willful ignorance, "there was nevertheless a reason why Mussolini's 'erudite' attribution of the saying was to Anaxagoras and not, for example, to Democritus or Plato; and this was the phonic similarity between *Anaxagoras* and *Protagoras*."[48] It was this pressure of banalization, rather than any unconscious motivation, that almost certainly led Freud from Signorelli to Boticelli.

And Boltraffio? Here again, philologists, paleographers, and textual critics possessed simple explanations for the slips that Freud attributed to unconscious forces. Boltraffio was an example of "disimprovement," when a scribe, recognizing that he has made a mistake, tries to correct himself—but corrects the wrong thing or corrects the right thing incorrectly. "Once the Boticelli 'slip' had occurred," Timpanaro explains,

> Freud takes his cue from it in an attempt to recover the correct name; and in the course of this attempted emendation he recalls the name of another Renaissance artist beginning with *Bo-* like *Boticelli*—namely, *Boltraffio*. In other words, he fails to isolate the element of the original word in which he effected an alteration, and thus instead of correcting the first part of it (*Bottic* to *Signor*), he takes the initial element (*Bo-*) to be right, and tries to correct the rest of it accordingly: nothing better than Boltraffio comes to mind.[49]

There was no need to refer to the unconscious. Freudian slips could be explained by material, cognitive, or institutional conditions. Timpanaro demonstrated the potentials of his method by reexamining another famous episode from *The Psychopathology of Everyday Life*, the so-called "aliquis" slip. Like the Signorelli slip, this one also involved a chance conversation on a train. Freud was chatting with a young man about a topic that concerned them both, the situation of the Jews in Austria. Growing agitated, the man burst out with the famous line from the *Aeneid* in which Dido curses her lover: "Exoriare aliquis nostris ex ossibus ultor" ("Come rising up from my bones, you avenger still unknown," in Fagles's translation). In reciting the line, however, Freud's companion forgot the word "aliquis" and reversed "nostris ex."

Naturally Freud suggested that the misquote must be a symptom of something and encouraged the young man to start associating. Following this chain of associations—aliquis, relics, saints, calendars; blood, liquid, flow—Freud offered the interpretation that the man was worried that his lover may be pregnant. Startled, the man conceded that yes indeed, he had just learned that his girlfriend had missed her period.

Was there a simpler explanation? Timpanaro found one: "Since this case concerns a young man who had been to school in Austria, it seems likely that he would have had a good recollection of elementary Latin prosody and metre, and would have kept up the habit of reading and reciting Latin hexameters according to the so-called *ictus* (rhythmic stresses) rather than the grammatical accents on individual words." This mode of recitation did not favor hexameters that began with pentasyllables (for example, "exoriare"), which in any case was an unusual construction in Augustan poetry. The young man was thus at a double disadvantage when it came to remembering Virgil's line: both the construction of the line and his educational background worked against it. "Had he gone to school in Italy," Timpanaro notes dryly, "this would have been less probable."[50] And what about the fact that Freud was right? That the young man was indeed worried about a pregnancy? Timpanaro responds that it is not a question of whether, after the slip, or even without it, the young man could be encouraged to confess his peccadilloes. This talent Freud shared with priests and cops. It was a matter of causation. It was simply implausible that the anxieties themselves caused the slip.

Timpanaro's critique has other elements that need not concern us here. For example, he repeatedly criticizes Freud's "antiempirical bias," which "may be said to attain its apotheosis in the work of Jung and, nearer our own time, in that of more lightweight figures such as Lévi-Strauss." At the same time, he mounts an energetic attack on the politics of psychoanalysis, noting, for example, that Freud never interprets slips as expressing a fear of social unrest or revolution, something that almost certainly would have been on the minds of many of his bourgeois patients in the Red Vienna of the 1920s and early 1930s. He offers this omission as evidence of the retrograde class allegiances of the psychoanalytic endeavor: "With the exception of some inspired but fairly restricted scientific conquests, psychoanalysis is neither a natural nor a human science, but a self-confession by the bourgeoisie of its own misery and perfidy, which blends the bitter insight and ideological blindness of a class in decline."[51] But even if these epistemological and political critiques were valid—they are not—they would hardly be as interesting or challenging as Timpanaro's philological one.

Withdrawal Slip

"Apart from being in debt," the young Freud confessed to his fiancé, Martha Bernays, "I know absolutely nothing about banking."[52] Of all the paperwork errors in *The Psychopathology of Everyday Life*, one stands out as especially undramatic. In the final months of 1900, Freud walked into the Austrian Post Office Savings Bank to withdraw 300 kronen to help a sick relative with medical expenses. Noticing that his account had 4,380 kronen, he decided he would withdraw an additional 80 kronen—that is to say, a total of 380 kronen—to bring the account down to a nice, round sum: 4,000 kronen. "After I had duly written out the check and cut off the figures corresponding to the sum, I suddenly noticed that I had not asked for 380 kronen as I intended, but for exactly 438 kronen, and took alarm at the unreliability of my conduct," he recounts. "I soon realized that my alarm was not called for; I was not now any poorer that I had been before. But it took me a good deal of reflection to discover what influence had disturbed my first intention, without making itself known to my consciousness."[53]

Without explanation, Freud offers this episode as one of the "more serious" examples of a slip of the pen.[54] He had already given us several less serious ones, including the time he switched October for September in his appointment book out of an unconscious wish to hasten a session with a particular patient, or the time he scrambled a reference to an obstetrician named Burck-hard, whose work he admired, out of hostility to another Burck-hard, who had written an unfavorable review of *The Interpretation of Dreams*. In later editions of *The Psychopathology of Everyday Life*, Freud also included several other examples of slips of the pen supplied by friends and colleagues. An American living in Europe, hoping to reconcile with his estranged wife, sent her a message pleading with her to book passage on the *Lusitania*. Fortunately, he caught his mistake in time to change the ship to the *Mauretania*, which had the distinct advantage of not having been sunk by the Germans in the war. But of course, he meant the *Lusitania*.

Freud's interpretation of the Post Office Savings Bank episode resembles his approach to the Signorelli and aliquis episodes, as well as many of his more "numerological" slips. At first he tries subtracting the sum he had intended to withdraw, 380 kronen, from the sum he actually withdrew, 438. He is left with the number 58, which means nothing to him. Reflecting further, he notices that the 438 kronen he had withdrawn was precisely 10 percent of the 4,380 kronen in the savings account. Now he was getting somewhere: 10 percent was the discount offered by booksellers to certain clients, and he had just been in an argu-ment with a bookseller. Freud had offered to sell back some used medical texts for 300 kronen, but the merchant demurred, saying that the asking price was high. If only the bookseller had bought the books! Freud would have recouped the exact sum that he was about to send to his sick relative. "There was no doubt that I regretted this expenditure," he remarks. "My affect on perceiv-ing my error can be understood as a fear of growing poor as a result of such expenditures. But both these feelings, my regret at the expenditure and my anxiety over becoming poor that was connected with it, was entirely foreign to my consciousness." "I should probably not have believed myself in any way capable of such an impulse," he concludes, "had I not had a dream a few days before which called for the same solution."[55]

Freud's footnote takes us to *On Dreams*, the abridged version of *The Interpretation of Dreams* that he had written at his publisher's request. The allusion is to the "Company at the Table d'Hôte" dream: Freud is sitting at a communal table eating spinach when the woman next to him begins caressing his leg. He brushes her off, but, undeterred, she complements the beauty of his eyes. The dream ends with a vague image of eyes or eyeglasses, he's not sure which. Freud returns to this dream repeatedly in *On Dreams*, approaching it from a number of directions, but stops before he actually reveals its secrets: "There are some which I should prefer to conceal from strangers."[56] In his meticulous reconstruction of Freud's self-analysis, Didier Anzieu suggests some of the problems troubling Freud at the time of the dream, including his friendship with Fliess, his treatment of the patient known as Dora, and his relationship with his sister-in-law Minna, who at that very moment was fighting tuberculosis in a sanatorium in Merano. She must have been the sick relative for whom the 300 kronen was destined.[57]

Timpanaro doesn't mention this Post Office Savings Bank episode, but we can imagine what he might have said about it. Freud's interpretation has the same arbitrariness that characterizes the rest of *The Psychopathology of Everyday Life*. At most, Freud was right about one thing: the sum he withdrew contained the same digits as the total amount in the account. Freud admits that he was distracted while performing the calculations and that he changed his mind at the last moment so that he could leave a nice, round sum in the account—an apparently obsessional preference left unanalyzed. The simplest and therefore best explanation is that faced with this proliferation of similar digits (4380, 300, 4080, 380, 4000, 438) he selected the figure (438) that most closely resembled the one right there in front of him (4380). This, too, could be ascribed to banalization. If Freud left off a zero, it was because he knew that he was withdrawing a three-digit sum. Once again, the answer was right there on the surface.

Indeed it is. We can't pose the question to Freud, of course, but we can pose it to the form itself, or at least one like it, from the archives of the Post Office Savings Bank (figure 8). Like many financial instruments, this withdrawal slip had redundancy built into it in order to prevent errors: the client writes out the sum in plain language and then indicates the sum a second time by making a series of incisions in a matrix provided for that purpose. The footnote in the *Standard Edition* explains it this way: "In Austria at the time, withdrawals from the Post Office Savings Bank involved cutting off portions of a sheet of paper printed with columns of digits: the point at which the cut was made indicated the number of kronen to be withdrawn."[58] The instructions on the back of the check use the term *abgeschnitten* ("cut away"); Freud's text uses a synonym, *ausgeschnitten*, which happens to carry the connotation of a low-cut dress. I have been unable to determine what sorts of scissors were used for this task, though we can assume that they were connected to the bank's counters by cords that were just a little too short.

At this point I encourage the reader to make a copy of the check so that she can reproduce Freud's error for herself. The form required a total of four cuts. Assuming Freud moved from top to bottom, that is, from the thousands to the ones column, he would have started by cutting through the top column entirely, whether he was intending to withdraw 380 or 438 kronen. From the form's perspective, there was no difference. The second cut, in the hundreds column, was supposed to signify a 3, but instead ended up with a 4. The difference here is a matter of a millimeter. Timpanaro might point out, rightly I think, that this error is best explained by external factors. Perhaps the scissors were dull or the form was jostled by a sudden draft of air.

This takes us to the third cut, in the tens column. Note that at this point, Freud might have thought that he had just marked a 3, as originally intended, and not a 4. In other words, it is possible that he was still aiming for 380. If this is the case, then the third cut would have been at the 8. But he makes the third cut at the 3, taking himself even further away from his conscious intention. From the form's perspective, the difference between a 3 and an

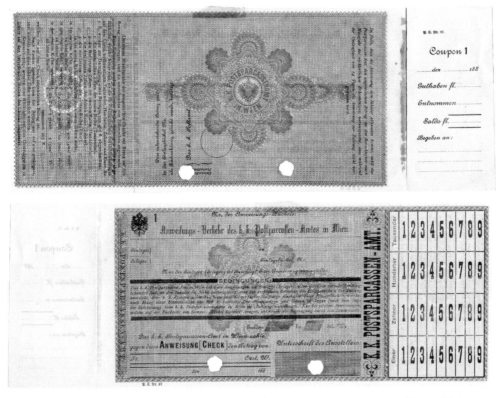

Figure 8. Withdrawal slip (recto/verso) from the Austrian Postal Savings Bank (ca. 1890) (courtesy of Wagner:Werk Museum Postparkasse, Vienna).

8 is much more significant than the difference between a 7 and an 8, say, or any other pair of sequential numbers. Imagine (or better still, try) manipulating the scissors. There are two ways of cutting the 8, and both require some care. Either Freud used the very tips of the scissors, which would have required him to position the scissors at the very edge of the form, or he cut at the fulcrum, which would have required a gentle touch to avoid cutting through to a 7, 6, or 5. To cut a 3 was easy by comparison, which is what exactly what he did.

It is still possible to believe that Freud was trying to withdraw 380 kronen but was obstructed by purely contingent factors. We could speculate, for example, that he remained unaware of the mistake in the second cut, believing he had made a 3 instead of a 4, and that the mistake in the third cut was pure clumsiness—he was preparing for a gentle cut at the fulcrum of the scissors, squeezed too hard, and ended up cutting past the 8 straight through to the 3. But wouldn't he have caught this? Another possibility is that the mistake between the 3 and the 4 in the second cut resulted from dull scissors and that the mistake between the 8 and the 3 in the third cut resulted from an attempt to compensate for that dullness. In other words, maybe Freud squeezed a bit too hard in the third cut, slicing right past the 8 to end up at the 3. But then again, if he was aware of the mistake in the second cut—whether its cause was clumsiness or dullness—he would have had to discard the form and start all over again. Instead, he continued on to the fourth cut: an unmistakable zero.

"It seems to me," Timpanaro writes, "that that the very simplicity and accessibility of the cases considered by Freud in *The Psychopathology* demonstrate in a particularly clear and direct way (even more so, for example, than those in *The Interpretation of Dreams*) the fragility of most of his explanations of them, and the basic defects of the method by which he arrived at these."[59] But perhaps even the simplest of these cases—withdrawing 438 kronen instead of 380—might be neither as simple nor as accessible as Timpanaro suggests. The difference between the two sums may be small, but the difference between the haptic experiences is substantial. Freud tells us that he wrote out the sum in the blank space before cutting it from the matrix; perhaps it was the other way around. Either way, he must have been quite attached to the number 438 in order to foil the redundancy measures encoded in the check. Whatever kind of failure it was, it was neither mechanical nor motor-cognitive.

Then again, perhaps it wasn't such a failure after all. Perhaps it was a success, if an unconscious one. Like the symptom or dream, the slip represents an attempt by the unconscious to get its message across—an attempt that is made difficult by repression, the primary processes, and any number of other measures taken by the ego to prevent embarrassment or worse. The question to ask is: What was being communicated? And the answer is: We don't know. We will never know. We can't know. Maybe Freud was daydreaming about books. Maybe, behind these daydreams, was a potent fantasy about sex with Minna, or with Dora, or with the fulsome young woman ahead of him on line—or with all three. Outside of the consulting room, we are unable to discover which, if any, of these possible causes it was; even inside the consulting room, it's very nearly impossible to be sure. But our inability to answer such questions conclusively does not relieve of us of our responsibility to pose them.

"Has critique run out of steam?" Bruno Latour asks.[60] If so, then we'll have to get out and push. After all, nobody ever said critique was going to be easy. The best we can do is to continue to read closely—sometimes very closely, magnifying glasses at the ready. And to continue to perfect a practice of reading that takes into account the labors of writing, whether those labors are oriented toward paperwork or some other, more esteemed object. It really does make a difference how a compositor's tray is organized, how a keyboard is laid out, how a form is designed, how a memo is worded. But we need to think more about what kind of difference this makes—how mistakes are made. No doubt sometimes, even most of the time, the mistakes will turn out to be a simple matter of semantic processing or cognitive-motor skills. But sometimes these won't be the simplest explanations, or sometimes the simplest explanations won't be the right ones. True, we will never gain access to the unconscious fantasies of some seventeenth-century printer or nineteenth-century clerk. And yet the practice of close reading might bring us a bit closer to their lives, frustrations, worries, if only in a partial and incomplete way, which is still better than no way at all.

From the Desk of Roland Barthes

Frustrations, worries, but also pleasures. There is a portrait of Roland Barthes is his office taken by Henri Cartier-Bresson in 1963 (figure 9). The photo is lovely, erotic even, especially in the sinuous line described by the bridge of the nose, the buttons of the collar and sweater, the crease of the pants. But it is the *studium* that, in its very unstudiedness, suggests how ideas take shape, how they become knowledge. We can see one of those midcentury wall units that were once merely functional and that are now merely decorative. From this perspective, at least, the shelves hold a few books and plenty of papers, sorted, stacked, filed horizontally and vertically. A ruler protrudes from an open cardboard box stuffed with still more scraps. Two wooden file boxes are latched shut. On top of them, alongside two more boxes that look as if they might contain microfilm, is a newspaper casually tossed aside; next to them is what appears to be a bottle of correction fluid and a replacement typewriter ribbon. Other photographs from the same session, taken from slightly different angles, reveal a transistor radio and an almost empty bottle of wine on the desk to Barthes's right. Barthes's office could be yours or mine, just tidier.

"Do you have a method of working?" the journalist Jean-Louis de Rambures asked Barthes in a 1973 interview for *Le Monde*. "It all depends on what you mean by method," Barthes replies. "As far as methodology is concerned, I have no opinion. But if you're talking about work habits..."[61] As he recounts his

Figure 9. Roland Barthes at his desk in 1963. Photograph by Henri Cartier-Bresson (courtesy of Magnum).

routines, we discover that the openness of his intellectual style is predicated on the exactness of his procedure. After describing in detail his preference for fountain pens over felt-tip or ballpoint, after recounting his experiments with the electric typewriter at the suggestion of Philippe Sollers, after detailing how he organizes his workplace and schedule in Paris and in the provinces, Barthes tells Rambures about his index-card system, which is based on slips of paper precisely one-quarter the size of his usual format: "At least that's how they were until the day standards were re-adjusted within the framework of European unification (in my opinion, one of the cruelest blows of the Common Market)."[62] We get the sense that he's joking, but only sort of.

Not long after Barthes's death in 1980, the journal *Communications* published a series of tributes to the critic. Perhaps the most unusual came from Jacques Le Goff, the great medieval historian, who had long served as president of the Sixth Section of the École Pratique des Hautes Études (now the École des Hautes Études en Sciences Sociales). Le Goff recounted how one of his first tasks upon becoming president had been to constitute the bureau, or central committee. It was a small committee, five people in all, who looked after the school's day-to-day affairs. But Le Goff believed that one person should be specially charged with the bigger picture, with the school's place in France and the world and the future. He decided to ask Barthes. "I didn't have much hope," Le Goff writes, "because I assumed that he would be completely devoted to his teaching, his writing. I couldn't imagine him taking on even the minimal amount of bureaucratic work that went along with this position."[63]

It turns out that Le Goff had underestimated him. After taking a few days to consider the request, Barthes agreed to a term of two years, nonrenewable. In fact, he served as a *membre du bureau* of the Sixth Section of the École Pratique des Hautes Études for two and a half years. For North American academics, this may not seem like much, but his French colleagues considered it an extraordinary gift. Evaluating student thesis proposals, overseeing the academic appeals process, revising university statutes, negotiating with union representatives—it turned out that the great theorist of the detail had an eye for it, as well. His famous sensitivity to language even extended to the minutes of the weekly meetings, where he routinely "replaced commas, selected more appropriate words, restored nuances, recalled the exact terms that had been used. Even in these humble texts he was never satisfied with platitudes or inexactitudes."[64]

The result could be funny or profound. Le Goff recalls meetings with ministerial functionaries who sat there, in awkward silence, as Barthes meticulously "read" through some proposal or another that they had brought with them. But it was at the regular committee meetings that he comported himself most magnificently. On Wednesday mornings, the committee would settle in to figure out this or that small matter pertaining to the school. "As we reviewed a page of the budget the epistemologist would suddenly awaken," Le Goff wrote. "Barthes used to say that he approved of dramatizing knowledge; he shared with us the pleasure of dramatizing paperwork.... For 'wilted' language he encouraged us to substitute 'fresh' language, and thus fresh thought. Seated there with his empty coffee cup, his overflowing ashtray, Roland, like a magician, would take us on a magic carpet ride around the offices." And so it went, for two and a half years, until Barthes moved to the Collège de France. "For two and a half years, as he performed his tasks, he was a man of justice, a poet, and a worker. Precise, discrete, and collegial."[65]

"Insignificance is the locus of true significance. This should never be forgotten," Barthes tells the interviewer from *Le Monde*. "That is why it seems so important to me to ask a writer about his writing habits, putting things on the most material level, I would even say the most minimal level possible. This is an anti-mythological action."[66] Here is the reductio ad minimum at its most minimalist.

142

Knowledge emerges out of arrangements and rearrangements of paper. Formats and protocols matter. Matter matters.

And yet... is there not something just a bit disingenuous about such explanations? I am reminded of the psychoanalyst Sándor Ferenczi's warning to parents about answering the child's question "Where do babies come from?" with a lesson in physiology. "It may be a good beginning, but it does not give full consideration to the internal needs and strivings of the child," Ferenczi writes. "It is interested, of course, in this question as it is interested in astronomy, but it is much more desirous of having the admission from parents and educators that the genital organ has a libidinous function, and as long as this is not admitted by the parents, no explanation is satisfactory."[67] There has been a trend, in some recent scholarship, to answer the question "Where do our thoughts come from?" with a similar literalism, which is to say, a similar evasiveness. Yes, it is "technically" true that our thoughts come from pens, papers, and desk drawers. But this only partially explains what we are up to when we produce even the most ordinary texts for the most mundane purposes.

Scattered throughout Barthes's reflections on his experience of writing we encounter another theme, not quite a subtext, more of a pretext, where "pre" here means something like the "pre" of Freud's "preconscious." If Barthes is an early adopter of the technical turn, he also warns us against taking him too literally. "I have often asked myself why I enjoy writing (manually, that is) to such a great extent," Barthes remarks in his introduction to Roger Druet's *La civilisation de l'écriture.* "As I write, my body shudders [*jouit*] with the pleasure of marking itself, inscribing itself, rhythmically, on the virgin surface (virginity being the infinitely possible).... Writing is not only a technical activity, it is also a bodily practice of *jouissance.*[68] I imagine that few, if any of us experience the bliss that Barthes associates with tracing words on a page. However, I also imagine that most, if not all of us derive some kind of satisfaction from a well-turned phrase, a persuasive argument, a felicitous speech act, even if it will only ever be read by some anonymous clerk in the Registrar's Office. In such texts, however briefly, however incompletely, we have the opportunity to fulfill fantasies of power and powerlessness, revenge and love. Any theory that purports to explain the technics of knowledge must take these fantasies into account.

The Wish-Utensil

In order to understand what a myth really is, must we choose
between platitude and sophism?
—Claude Lévi-Strauss, "The Structural Study of Myth"

"The government's laws and orders will be transmitted to the
furthest reaches of the social order with the speed of electric
fluid."[1] Such was the promise made by the chemist, industrialist,
and minister of the interior Jean-Antoine Chaptal in 1800 as he
announced the creation of France's modern administrative institutions. The idea of the paperless office was born.

Media historians and theorists have long recognized the
astounding affordability, versatility, portability, and durability of
paper, which is in many respects the ideal material support. As
a corollary, the paperless office has been dismissed as a "myth"
by social scientists, information engineers, and corporate con-
sultants alike, who predict that paper's many advantages will
continue to make it indispensable for the foreseeable future.[2]
Myth it may be, but not (or at least not only) in the simple
sense that is typically employed in these contexts. The paperless
office should also be interpreted as a myth in the Lévi-Straussian
sense, that is to say, an imaginary resolution to paperwork's many
contradictions.

Will the computer ever replace paperwork? Or will it turn
out to be another one of those "wish-utensils for acquiring what
is not available" that feature so prominently in so many of our

fairy tales? The phrase is Ernst Bloch's in *The Principle of Hope*. "Wishful gadgets of the handiest kind offer themselves to the weak, magically," he notes. The walking stick that turns into a divining rod, the sack that refills itself with food, the lamp that conceals a magic genie. "Wish becomes command, the effort of doing things drops away.... In general, technological-magical treasure-hunting is the fairytale aspect itself in this kind of fairy tale."[3]

In 1967, IBM commissioned a short film called *The Paperwork Explosion*. The film, which promoted the IBM MT/ST, was directed by a then little-known experimental filmmaker named Jim Henson and scored by Raymond Scott, the composer and inventor who wrote most of the tunes behind Looney Tunes, introduced the first racially integrated network studio orchestra, and pioneered electronic music with such technologies as the Orchestra Machine, the Clavivox, and the Electronium. Henson and Scott's collaboration explains, no doubt, the film's considerable formal intelligence and narrative wit.[4]

The MT/ST, released in 1964, combined the company's Selectric typewriter with a magnetic tape disk. Operators entered text and formatting codes onto magnetic tape; they could then make simple changes before printing a clean copy of the document. More advanced versions of the machine included two tape drives, allowing for mail merges and similar features. Among historians of computing, the MT/ST is best known as the first machine to be marketed as a "word processor" (a term that, as Thomas Haigh has pointed out, emerged at the same moment as Cuisinart's "food processor").[5]

The IBM film opens with an extraordinary montage of the history of media and communication: scribes and printing presses, water mills and assembly lines, container ships and spacecraft. This montage is interrupted by the sound of brakes squealing and the image of a car swerving toward the viewer. Cut to a rural scene, the sound of chickens, an old man with a corncob pipe. "Well," he says. "You can't stop progress." A quick glimpse of a

subway train before a man who looks like he must be an engineer
of some kind tells us "It's not a question of stopping it so much
as just keeping up with it." An image of a jetliner before another
talking head—thick frames, thin tie—tells us that "at IBM our
work is related to the paperwork explosion." Suddenly, stacks of
paper on a desk explode into the air and sail through a blue sky.
Cut to an office, where we see paperwork exploding in the more
metaphorical sense, spilling out of desks and drawers. Cut back to
the stacks of paper tumbling through the sky. "Paperwork explosion," a voice says.

We are not quite one minute into the five-minute film. Faces
of office workers appear one after the other to tell us "There's
always been a lot of paperwork in an office—but today there's
more than ever before—there's more than ever before—certainly
more than there used to be!" This last statement is spoken by
the old farmer, whose folksy observation also concludes the next
montage: "In the past, there always seemed to be enough time and
people to do the paperwork—there always seemed to be enough
time to do the paperwork—there always seemed to be enough
people to do the paperwork—there always seemed to be enough
time and people to do the paperwork—but today there isn't."
The pulse of Raymond Scott's electronic music accelerates as
more faces speak to us of their struggles with paperwork: "Today
everyone has to spend more time on paperwork: management
has to spend more time on paperwork—secretaries have to spend
more time on paperwork—companies have to spend more time on
paperwork—salesmen—brokers—engineers—accountants—lawyers—supervisors—doctors—executives—teachers—office man-
agers—bankers—foremen—bookkeepers—everybody has to
spend more time on paperwork." Once again we see a shot of
paperwork exploding. The farmer: "Seems to me we could use
some help."

Fortunately, help is available. We see businessmen chattering excitedly about rumors of a new machine from IBM. "With
IBM dictation equipment, I can get four times as much thinking

recorded as I can by writing it down and twice as much as I can by dictating to highly skilled secretary." The camera reveals a series of futuristic-looking electronic components as voices talk about cordless dictation and error-free copy. Then a new series of faces and voices: "IBM machines can do the work—so that people have time to think—machines should do the work—that's what they're best at—people should do the thinking—that's what they're best at." Once again the music accelerates as these faces and voices speed across the screen: "Machines should work—people should think—machines—should work—people—should think—machines—should—work—people—should—think."

The Paperwork Explosion takes its place in a long history of images of paperwork combusting. Think of J. M. W. Turner's two canvases Burning of the Houses of Parliament (1835). These fires weren't sparked by paperwork, exactly, but by the notched wood sticks used for some eight centuries by the Exchequer's office to record receipts and expenditures. As Charles Dickens recounted twenty years later: "The sticks were housed in Westminster, and it would naturally occur to any intelligent person that nothing could be easier than to allow them to be carried away for firewood by the miserable people who lived in that neighborhood. However, they never had been useful, and official routine required that they should never be, and so the order went out that they were to be privately and confidentially burned."[6] The sticks were thus unceremoniously fed to a furnace in the basement of the House of Lords on October 16, 1834. They took their revenge, however, by taking the Houses of Lords and Commons with them into the flames. Turner's paintings depict the accident in delirious detail.[7]

Think also of the paperwork explosion that opens the narrative of Werner Fassbinder's The Marriage of Maria Braun (1979). As the film opens, we hear bombs falling and watch a wall collapse to reveal a wedding in progress. The bride and groom and guests scramble to get out of the Civil Registry Office as women scream and babies cry and hundreds and hundreds of documents tumble through the air. "Sign here! Put a stamp on it!" Maria Braun yells to the Nazi official as they lie prostrate on the ground. A similar image reappears several years later in Terry Gilliam's *Brazil* (1985), as Robert De Niro's character vanishes beneath paperwork falling from the sky following the destruction of the Ministry of Information.

The "paperwork explosion" expresses both a threat and a wish. The threat, an old one, is that we are being overwhelmed by paperwork's proliferation, its explosion.[8] The wish is to convert all this cumbersome matter into liberating energy, which is exactly what explosions do. From Chaptal's "electric fluid" to IBM's "machines should work, people should think" to USA.gov's slogan "Government Made Easy," we remain attached to the idea that someday, somehow, we can liberate this energy, put it to other uses.

Significantly, in IBM's *The Paperwork Explosion*, the liberation of this energy ends up being the liberation of labor. This becomes apparent at the very end, when we discover that our farmer is not exactly a farmer after all, but has returned from the future to deliver his message. "So I don't do too much work anymore," he tells us. "I'm too busy thinking." The camera fades to black as we hear a harmonica playing in the background, a striking contrast to the electronic pulses and clattering machinery that have provided the soundtrack so far. In the future, machines work while people think. This is the old utopian dream of a government of men replaced by the administration of things (or of bits of data). This is man who has been hunting in the morning, fishing in the afternoon, herding in the evening, philosophizing after dinner, surfing the web late into the night, without having become a hunter, fisherman, herdsman, philosopher, or coder. This is man unalienated. Not bad results from a business machine.

Yet we must not miss the ambiguity here. "Machines should work, people should think." The message repeats itself several times; it's the core of the film's techno-utopian vision. We can imagine IBM executives and lawyers and public-relations agents sitting across a table from the thirty-year-old Jim Henson reminding him to make sure he includes these lines in his film. What if we shifted the emphasis just a little bit? From "*machines* should *work, people* should *think*" to "machines *should* work, people *should* think"? Is it possible that the film might be trying to warn us against its own techno-utopianism? Read this way, the film is less an imaginary resolution to the problem of information overload in the modern era than an imaginative critique of this imaginary resolution. Machines should work, but they frequently don't; people should think, but in this day and age, they seldom have the time.

Acknowledgments

This book is still, in many ways, a student work, which is to say, the work of my teachers. Most of its preoccupations—writing, ideology, state apparatuses, the unconscious—emerged from undergraduate seminars with Nancy Armstrong, Michael Silverman, Leonard Tennenhouse, and Elizabeth Weed. As a graduate student, I benefitted from the high spirits and even higher standards of Keith Baker, Mary Louise Roberts, Paul Robinson, Colin Jones, James Sheehan, and Hans Ulrich Gumbrecht. I would especially like to thank Lou Roberts, who understood what I was trying to do long before I did.

At the Princeton Society of Fellows, I had the great good fortune of working with Leonard Barkan and Michael Wood, who were as brilliant, witty, and generous as their prose would lead one to believe. Teaching and talking with Anthony Grafton and Carla Hesse opened up new possibilities for the project. Hal Foster helped me find a publisher. My fellow fellows, including Sunil Agnani, Christopher Bush, Bianca Finzi-Contini Calabresi, Anne-Maria Makhulu, Gayle Salamon, and Martin Scherzinger, contributed to a rethinking of many of the themes. I would also like to thank Esther da Costa Meyer, Robert Darnton, Phil Nord, Carol Rigolot, François Rigolot, and Nigel Smith for their interest and support. Mary Harper deserves a special thanks for always making everything, even already very good things, better.

A fellowship from the School of Social Science of the Institute for Advanced Study stimulated another rethinking of this project in 2009–10. A fellowship from the Internationales Kolleg für Kulturtechnikforschung und Medienphilosophie (IKKM Weimar) in summer 2012 made it possible for me to complete the manuscript. Other funding came from the Franco-American (Fulbright) Commission, the Social Science Research Council, and the Mrs. Giles Whiting Foundation; travel grants were provided by Stanford, Princeton, New York University, and the Society for French Historical Studies. Research for the book was undertaken at the Archives Nationales, the Bibliothèque Nationale de France, the Bibliothèque Historique de la Ville de Paris, the Bibliothèque Administrative de la Ville de Paris, the New York Public Library, and the libraries at Stanford, Princeton, Columbia, and New York University. My thanks to all of these institutions, and their paperworkers, for their support. Thanks, too, to Monika Wenzl-Bachmayer and the Wagner:Werk Museum Postparkasse in Vienna for the cover image.

Early attempts at this book were presented at seminars and conferences at the Center for Global Culture and Communication, Northwestern; the Clark Memorial Library, UCLA; the Center for Cultural Analysis, Rutgers; the Workshop on Material Texts, University of Pennsylvania; the Center for Eighteenth-Century Studies, University of Indiana-Bloomington; the European History Workshop, Cornell; the Workshop on Print, Agency, and Interaction, McGill; the Radcliffe Institute for Advanced Study, Harvard; the Beinecke Rare Book and Manuscript Library, Yale; and the Columbia University Seminar in Media Theory and History. As I revised the book, I often found myself wishing that I had taken better notes on some of the wonderful exchanges that I had at these events; I'm sure many errors and omissions could have been avoided.

I would also like to thank my colleagues at NYU for their help, especially Lily Chumley, Gabriella Coleman, Alexander Galloway, Stefanos Geroulanos, Lisa Gitelman, A. B. Huber, Eric Klinenberg, Ted Magder, Susan Murray, Michael Ralph, Martin Scherzinger, John Shovlin, Clifford Siskin, Helga Tawil-Souri,

Aurora Wallace, and Caitlin Zaloom. A casual conversation on the subway with Emily Apter has turned into an enduring friendship and collaboration. Marissa Kantor Dennis has been a splendid research assistant, copyeditor, interlocutor, and friend. Beyond NYU, the book has benefitted in ways big and small from conversations with Nicholas Basbanes, Alan Bass, Ann Blair, Éloïse Brezault, Kate Cambor, Arianne Chernock, Jim Clark, Amy Freund, Paul Haacke, Graeme Hoffman, Andrew Jainchill, Toby Jones, Shu Kuge, Daniel Lee, Alison MacKeen, Rebecca Manley, Cecily Marcus, Michael Moskowitz, Sina Najafi, John Paton, Leah Price, James Ryerson, Emmanuel Saadia, Daniel Sherman, Dana Simmons, Matthew Noah Smith, Judi Stevens, Judith Surkis, Meredith TenHoor, Anoush Terjanian, Anthony Vidler, Martha Zuber, the Coe family, and my co-editors at *History of the Present*. A sincere thanks to Judith Butler for helping me find a way to finish the book.

My editor, Jonathan Crary, has been one of my idols since I first worked my way through *Techniques of the Observer* my freshman year in college. How fortunate I was to be able to work with him. Also at Zone Books, Meighan Gale and Gus Kiley were extraordinarily patient and precise—and I didn't make it easy. If you're holding the actual book in your actual hands, you can appreciate the talents of Julie Fry, the designer. Bud Bynack's copyediting was also a wonder to behold. Earlier versions of bits and pieces of this book have appeared as "The Demon of Writing: Paperwork, Public Safety, and the Reign of Terror," *Representations* 98 (Spring 2007); "Hunting the Plumed Mammal: The History of 'Bureaucracy' in France," in Peter Becker and Rüdiger von Krosigk, eds., *Figures of Authority: Contributions Towards a Cultural History of Governance* (Peter Lang, 2008); "From the Desk of Roland Barthes: Putting *Mater* (and *Pater*) back in Materialism," *West 86th* 18.2 (fall 2011); and "Paperwork Explosion," *West 86th* online. Thanks to all the editors and reviewers for their advice and assistance.

The introduction presents Joan Scott as the book's intellectual superego; in truth, she's the source of its drives, and has been for over fifteen years. I have also been driven (and sometimes carried) by Erica Robles-Anderson, Charly Coleman, A. B. Huber, Yael Kropsky, Jessica Levin, Tom Levin, Camille Robcis, Milena Kropsky Robcis, Gayle Salamon, Nicole Stahlmann, and Jamieson Webster. My brother and sister, parents and grandparents, and other, harder-to-define kin have kept me going. And then there is J. L., without whom this book would have remained a repetition of Freudian *Hilflosigkeit* rather than a reflection on it.

This book, and its author, are dedicated to Julie Coe.

Notes

INTRODUCTION: THE PSYCHIC LIFE OF PAPERWORK

1. Michael Herzfeld, *The Social Production of Indifference: Exploring the Symbolic Roots of Western Bureaucracy* (Chicago: University of Chicago Press, 1992), p. 7.

2. Jacques Derrida, *Of Grammatology*, trans. Gayatri Chakravorty Spivak (Baltimore: Johns Hopkins University Press, 1976), p. 17.

3. Joan Scott, "Against Eclecticism," *differences: A Journal of Feminist Cultural Studies* 16.3 (2005), p. 116.

4. Bruno Latour, *La fabrique du droit: Une ethnographie du Conseil d'État* (Paris: La Découverte, 2002), pp. 83–84, my translation.

5. Ben Kafka, "Paperwork: The State of the Discipline," *Book History* 12 (2009). For a more recent, more extensive review of the literature, see Matthew S. Hull, "Documents and Bureaucracy," *Annual Review of Anthropology* 41 (2012), pp. 251–67.

6. Barbara Johnson, *Persons and Things* (Cambridge, MA: Harvard University Press, 2008), p. 3.

7. Friedrich Nietzsche, *Thus Spake Zarathustra*, trans. R. J. Hollingdale (New York: Penguin, 2003), p. 76.

8. Hannah Arendt, *Eichmann in Jerusalem: A Report on the Banality of Evil* (New York: Penguin, 1994), p. 289.

9. Judith Butler, *The Psychic Life of Power: Theories in Subjection* (Stanford: Stanford University Press, 1997); Lydia H. Liu, *The Freudian Robot: Digital Media and the Future of the Unconscious* (Chicago: University of Chicago Press, 2010).

10. Freud said he was "amused" by the comparison, but also slipped over

the reviewer's name and nationality. Sigmund Freud, *Group Psychology and the Analysis of the Ego* (1921), in *The Standard Edition of the Complete Psychological Works of Sigmund Freud*, ed. and trans. James Strachey, 24 vols. (London: Hogarth, 1953–1973), vol. 18, p. 128.

11. Perry Meisel and Walter M. Kendrick (eds.), *Bloomsbury/Freud: The Letters of James and Alix Strachey* (New York: Basic Books, 1985), p. 332.

12. Joan W. Scott, "The Incommensurability of Psychoanalysis and History," *History and Theory* 51.1 (February 2012), p. 68.

13. The classic statement of this position on interpretation is Otto Fenichel, *The Problem of Psychoanalytic Technique* (New York: Psychoanalytic Quarterly Press, 1941). See also André Green, "Surface Analysis, Deep Analysis (The Role of the Preconscious in Psychoanalytic Technique)," *The International Review of Psychoanalysis* 1.4 (1974), pp. 415–23; Fred Busch, "A Shadow Concept," *The International Review of Psychoanalysis* 87.6 (2006), pp. 1471–85.

14. Jacques Lacan, *The Seminar of Jacques Lacan, Book VII: Ethics of Psychoanalysis, 1959–1960*, trans. Dennis Porter (New York: Norton, 1992), pp. 61–62.

15. M. J. Mavidal and M. E. Laurent (eds.), *Archives parlementaires de 1787 à 1860*, 1st series, 96 vols. (Paris: P. Dupont / CNRS, 1867–present), vol. 57, p. 599 (January 22, 1793).

CHAPTER ONE: THE DISCIPLINED STATE

1. The case is recounted in the *Mémoire sur les privilèges des avocats. Dans lequel on traite du Tableau et de la Discipline de l'Ordre. Pour Me. Morizot, Avocat au Parlement, contre M. le Procureur-Général* (1785). This brief, which was written by Ambroise Falconnet, is reprinted in the second volume of Ambroise Falconnet, *Le barreau français, partie moderne*, 2 vols. (Paris, 1806–1808). Falconnet's intervention in this case is situated in its corporate context by David A. Bell, *Lawyers and Citizens: The Making of a Political Elite in Old Regime France* (Oxford: Oxford University Press, 1994), pp. 169–71.

2. On the primacy of the discourses of will, justice, and reason in Old Regime political culture, see Keith Michael Baker, *Inventing the French Revolution: Essays in the Political Culture of the Eighteenth Century* (Cambridge: Cambridge University Press, 1994).

3. Walter Benjamin, *The Arcades Project*, trans. Howard Eiland and Kevin McLaughlin (Cambridge, MA: Harvard University Press, 1999), p. 4.

4. M. Guillaute, *Mémoire sur la réformation de la police de France soumis au roi en 1749* (Paris: Hermann, 1974). On Saint-Aubin's contribution to Guillaute's treatise, see Colin B. Baily et al., *Gabriel de Saint-Aubin, 1724–1780*, exhibition catalogue (New York: Frick Collection / Musée du Louvre, 2007).

5. On Ramelli, see Lisa Jardine and Anthony Grafton, "Studied for Action: How Gabriel Harvey Read His Livy," *Past and Present* 129 (November 1990), p. 46. We catch a glimpse of similar, though smaller machines being employed in the Stasi archives in the film *The Lives of Others*, directed by Florian Henckel von Donnersmarck (2006).

6. Leora Auslander, *Taste and Power: Furnishing Modern France* (Berkeley: University of California Press, 1996), p. 35.

7. See the reconsideration in François R. Velde and David R. Weir, "The Financial Market and Government Debt Policy in France, 1746–1793," *Journal of Economic History* 52.1 (March 1992).

8. Thomas Ertman, *Birth of the Leviathan: Building States and Regimes in Early Modern Europe* (Cambridge: Cambridge University Press, 1997), p. 32.

9. Edme-Etienne Morizot, *Dénonciation à l'Assemblée nationale contre ses bureaux du Comité des rapports* (n.p, n.d.), p. 4. A note in ink in the copy of this pamphlet conserved at the Bibliothèque Historique de la Ville de Paris indicates May 26, 1790.

10. Gabriel-Joseph-Xavier Ricard de Sealt also served as a *subdélégué de l'intendant* in Aix prior to the Revolution. He was a member of the Jacobin Club until July 1791, when he joined the Feuillants. He was elected to the Convention and dispatched on mission to the Italian campaign, but during his voyage, he was captured by corsairs and taken to Majorca, where he spent the next twenty-eight months in captivity. He returned to France in 1796 and occupied various administrative posts, including prefect of the Isère from 1800 until his death in 1802. See Edna Hindie Lemay, *Dictionnaire des constituants, 1789–1791*, 2 vols. (Paris: Universitas, 1991), s.v. "Ricard de Sealt."

11. Morizot, *Dénonciation à l'Assemblée nationale*, p. 10.

12. Morizot angrily protested this transfer in a letter: "If your gentlemen, who are not at all familiar with my affair, had done me the grace of calling on me, they would have judged differently after hearing me. To know an affair it is not sufficient to look at a few of the bricks. It is necessary to enter entirely into the documents and to reflect on them, and even then one will frequently

make mistakes. It is not surprising that, having neither examined nor delved more deeply into the affair, the committee has made a mistake. Forgive me this observation, because it is just and because for thirteen months now the deputies have had me running this way and that without advancing, and a complaint is at least permitted to me while I suffer since I am without bread." Edme-Etienne Morizot, letter dated May 29, 1790, Archives Nationales, Comité des rapports. D XXIX 89.

13. *Ibid.*

14. M. J. Mavidal and M. E. Laurent (eds.), *Archives parlementaires de 1787 à 1860*, 1st series, 96 vols. (Paris: P. Dupont / CNRS, 1867–present), vol. 16, p. 692 (July 3, 1790).

15. *Ibid.*

16. *Ibid.*

17. Archives Nationales. DXXIX bis 34 doss. 357 item 1. Comité des Recherches, "Emploi des Cents Soixante treize mille six cens livres touchées au tresor royal sur les demands de M. de LaFayette." The information about why Morizot was being followed comes from Pierre Caillet and Nicole Michel-Dansac, *Comité des Recherches de l'Assemblée nationale, 1789–1791: Inventaire analytique de la sous-série D XXIX bis* (Paris: Archives Nationales, 1993), p. 561.

18. Edme-Étienne Morizot, *Appel au roi, en présence de la nation et sous les yeux de l'Europe, d'un deni de justice de l'Assemblée nationale* (Paris, 1790), pp. 65–66.

19. *Ibid.*, p. 64.

20. When the editors of the fiercely counterrevolutionary journal *L'Ami du Roi* reported on the debate over Morizot's case in the National Assembly, they found nothing interesting about the case, merely reminding their readers that the Reports Committee was favored by the Assembly's "left side." *L'Ami du Roi, des François, de l'Ordre, et sur-tout de la Vérité, par les continuateurs de Fréron* 35 (July 5, 1790).

21. Lemay, *Dictionnaire des constituants*, s.v. "Ricard de Séalt."

22. Morizot, *Appel au roi*, p. 126.

23. Morizot, *Dénonication à l'Assemblée nationale*, p. 2.

24. Thomas Hobbes, *Leviathan* (Cambridge: Cambridge University Press, 1996), p. 156.

25. Lucien Bély, *Dictionnaire de l'Ancien Régime: Royaume de France:*

XVIe–XVIIIe siècle (Paris: Presses Universitaires de France, 1996), s.v. "archives."

26. Charles François Toustain and René Prosper Tassin, *Nouveau traité de diplomatique: Où l'on examine les fondemens de cet art: on établit des règles sur le discernement des titres, et l'on expose historiquement les caractères des bulles pontificales et des diplômes donnés en chaque siècle: avec des éclaircissemens sur un nombre considérable de points d'histoire, de chronologie, de critique & de discipline . . . par deux religieux Bénédictins de la Congrégation de S. Maur* (Paris: Chez G. Desprez; P.-G. Cavelier, 1750–1765), p. 407.

27. Denis Diderot and Jean Le Rond d'Alembert (eds.), *Encyclopédie, ou Dictionnaire raisonné des sciences, des arts et des métiers*, 17 vols. (Paris, 1751–65), s.v. "diplôme & diplômatique."

28. Alexis de Tocqueville, *The Old Regime and the Revolution*, trans. Alan S. Kahan (Chicago: University of Chicago Press, 1998), pp. 200–201, translation modified.

29. John Markoff, "Governmental Bureaucratization: General Processes and an Anomalous Case," *Comparative Studies in Society and History* 17.4 (October 1975); Gilbert Simon and John Markoff (eds.), *Revolutionary Demands: A Content Analysis of the Cahiers de Doléances of 1789* (Stanford: Stanford University Press, 1998), p. 248.

30. Jean-Jacques Rousseau, "Of the Social Contract," in *The Social Contract and Other Later Political Writings*, trans. Victor Gourevitch (Cambridge: Cambridge University Press, 1997), p. 115.

31. On Sieyès's contribution to the formation representative government in the French Revolution, in addition to the book by Keith Baker cited above, see Paul Friedland, *Political Actors: Representative Bodies and Theatricality in the Age of the French Revolution* (Ithaca: Cornell University Press, 2002); Pasquale Pasquino, *Sieyès et l'invention de la constitution en France* (Paris: Odile Jacob, 1998); Pierre Rosanvallon, *Le peuple introuvable: Histoire de la représentation démocratique en France* (Paris: Gallimard, 1998); William H. Sewell, Jr., *A Rhetoric of Bourgeois Revolution: The Abbé Sieyès and "What Is the Third Estate?"* (Durham: Duke University Press, 1994); Michael Sonenscher, *Before the Deluge: Public Debt, Inequality, and the Intellectual Origins of the French Revolution* (Princeton: Princeton University Press, 2007).

32. Emmanuel-Joseph Sieyès, "Observations sur le rapport du Comité du

constitution concernant la nouvelle organisation de la France," in Emmanuel-Joseph Sieyès, *Écrits politiques*, ed. Robert Zapperi (Brussels: Éditions des Archives Contemporaries, 1994), p. 262.

33. Jean-Jacques Rousseau, "Political Economy," in *The Social Contract and Other Later Political Writings*, p. 26, translation modified.

34. Jacques Derrida, *Of Grammatology*, trans. Gayatri Chakravorty Spivak (Baltimore: Johns Hopkins University Press, 1976), ch. 2.

35. Though written first, it was published second, between the *Essay on Privileges* and *What Is the Third Estate?*, and went through two editions. Paul Bastid, *Sieyès et sa pensée* (Paris: Hachette, 1970), p. 55.

36. Emmanuel-Joseph Sieyès, "Views of the Executive Means Available to the Representatives of France in 1789," in Sieyès, *Political Writings: Including the Debate Between Sieyès and Tom Paine in 1791*, trans. Michael Sonenscher (Indianapolis: Hackett, 2003), pp. 7 and 16.

37. *Ibid.*, p. 46

38. *Ibid.*, p. 48.

39. C. B. Macpherson, *The Political Theory of Posessive Individualism* (Oxford: Oxford University Press, 1962), pp. 195 and 251.

40. Sieyès, "Views of the Executive Means Available to the Representatives of France in 1789," pp. 48–49.

41. Georges Lefebvre, *La Grande Peur de 1789* (Paris: Armand Colin, 1970), p. 114.

42. Colin Jones, *The Great Nation: France from Louis XV to Napoleon* (London: Penguin, 2002), p. 419.

43. This report, by Amelot, secretaire d'état, is reproduced in Frantz Funck-Brentano, *Les archives de la Bastille: La formation du dépôt* (Paris: Dole, 1890), p. 5. I am relying on his brief study for the following account.

44. [Charpentier or Manuel], *La Bastille dévoilée, ou Recueil de pièces authentiques pour servir à son histoire*, 9 vols. (Paris: Desenne, 1789), vol. 1, p. 9.

45. *Ibid.*, pp. 1, 8, 12.

46. Mavidal and Laurent (eds.), *Archives parlementaires de 1787 à 1860*, vol. 8, pp. 345–46 (August 4, 1789).

47. François Furet, *La Révolution française de Turgot à Napoleon (1770–1814)* (Paris: Hachette, 1988), p. 125.

48. These hours were announced in the *Almanach royal, année 1792* (Paris:

D'Houry, 1792), p. 177. On the formation of the archives, see Krzysztof Pomian, "Les archives: Du trésor des chartes au CARAN," in Pierre Nora (ed.), *Les lieux de mémoire*, vol. 3, *Les France* (Paris: Gallimard, 1992).

49. Charles Tilly, *Coercion, Capital, and European States, AD 990–1992* (Oxford: Blackwell, 1992), pp. 107–108.

50. Edna Hindie Lemay, "La composition de l'Assemblée nationale constituante: Les hommes de la continuité," *Revue d'histoire moderne et contemporaine* 29.3 (July–September 1977), pp. 341–63.

51. Emmanuel-Joseph Sieyès, *Quelques idées de Constitution applicables à la Ville de Paris. En juillet 1789* (Versailles: Baudouin, n.d.), p. 29.

52. It is all but ignored, for example, by the contributors to Dale Van Kley (ed.), *The French Idea of Freedom: The Old Regime and the Declaration of Rights of 1789* (Stanford: Stanford University Press, 1994). There is a brief discussion of it in Marcel Gauchet, *La révolution des droits de l'homme* (Paris: Gallimard, 1989), pp. 183–85. The most extensive examination of which I am aware is Laurent Richer's chapter in Gérard Conac, Marc Debene, and Gérard Teboul (eds.), *La déclaration des droits de l'homme et du citoyen du 1789: Histoire, analyse et commentaires* (Paris: Economica, 1993).

53. Max Ferrand (ed.), *The Records of the Federal Convention of 1787*, 4 vols. (New Haven: Yale University Press, 1911), vol. 2, p. 618.

54. See Philip Dawson, "Le 6e bureau de l'Assemblée nationale et son project de Déclaration des droits de l'homme," in *Annales historiques de la Révolution française* (April–June 1978), as well as the introduction to Antoine de Baecque (ed.), *L'an 1 des droits de l'homme* (Paris: Presses du CNRS, 1988).

55. Emmanuel-Joseph Sieyès, "Préliminaire de la Constitution: Reconaissance et exposition des droits de l'homme et du citoyen. Lu les 20 et 21 juillet 1789 au Comité de Constitution," in Christine Fauré (ed.), *Les déclarations des droits de l'homme de 1789*, new ed. (Paris: Payot, 1992), p. 109.

56. Jean Joseph Mounier, "Projet des premiers articles de la Constitution, lu dans la séance du 28 juillet 1789," in Fauré (ed.), *Les déclarations*, p. 115. According to the *Archives Parlementaires*, the project was actually presented on the July 27.

57. Jacques-Guillaume Thouret, "Projet de déclaration des droits de l'homme en société," in Fauré (ed.), *Les déclarations*, p. 156.

58. Emmanuel-Joseph Sieyès, "Déclaration des droits du citoyen français,

détachée du préliminaire de la Constitution" (August 12, 1789), in Fauré (ed.), *Les déclarations*, p. 252.

59. See de Baecque (ed.), *L'an 1 des droits de l'homme*, p. 31.

60. "Projet de déclaration des droits de l'homme et du citoyen discuté dans le sixième Bureau de l'Assemblée nationale," in Fauré (ed.), *Les déclarations*, p. 257.

61. The debate took place on August 26, 1789. It is reconstructed in de Baecque (ed.), *L'an 1 des droits de l'homme*, pp. 190–94.

62. These statistics and the committee's organization come from the *Rapport présenté à l'Assemblée nationale, par les inspecteurs des secrétariats des comités & des bureaux* (Paris: Imprimerie Nationale, 1791), p. 19.

63. *Ibid.*, p. 19.

64. Pierre Victurnien Vergniaud, *Rapport de M. Vergniaud sur l'état des travaux de l'Assemblée-Nationale-Constituante au 30 Septembre 1791* (Paris: Imprimerie Nationale, 1791), p. 29.

65. *Rapport présenté*, p. 19.

66. *Almanach royal, année 1791* (Paris: D'Houry, 1791), pp. 132–33.

67. *Ibid.*, p. 134.

68. *Ibid.*

69. Edme-Etienne Morizot, *Placet à la reine, en invoquant l'attention des augustes maisons de Bourbon et d'Autriche, sur la justice qui émanera du trone* (n.p, n.d.), p. 7.

70. *Ibid.*, p. 20.

71. Edme-Etienne Morizot, *Placet au citoyen Rolland, ministre de l'interieur, contre le citoyen Boullanger, juge de paix de la section des Gardes-Françaises, ci-devant l'Oratoire* (n.p., n.d.), p. 11.

72. *Ibid.*, p. 9.

73. *L'Ami du Peuple*, October 8, 1792, in Jean-Paul Marat, *Oeuvres politiques, 1789–1793*, ed. Jacques de Cock and Charlotte Goëtz, 10 vols. (Brussels: Pôle Nord, 1995), vol. 8, pp. 4864–65.

74. *Ibid.*

CHAPTER TWO: THE DEMON OF WRITING

1. Charles-Guillaume Étienne and Alphonse-Louis-Dieudonné Martainville, *Histoire du théâtre français depuis le commencement de la révolution jusqu'à*

la réunion générale, 4 vols. (Paris: Chez Barba, An X–1802), vol. 3, pp. 146–48.

2. *Journal des Débats et Loix du Pouvoir Legislatif et des Actes du Gouvernement*, 5 Messidor Year X (June 23, 1802), pp. 2–3.

3. *Courrier des Spectacles*, 24 Germinal Year XI (April 14, 1803). Cited in Arthur Pougin, *La Comédie Française et la Révolution: Scènes, récits et notices* (Paris: Gaultier, Magnier, & Cie., n.d. [1902]), p. 163.

4. On dancing, see Ronald Schechter, "Gothic Thermidor: The Bals des victimes, the Fantastic, and the Production of Historical Knowledge in Post-Terror France," *Representations* 61 (Winter 1998). The Terror's role in the formation of modern liberalism is one of the principal themes, for example, of François Furet, *Revolutionary France, 1770–1880* (Oxford: Blackwell, 1995). For a compelling critique of the use of psychological categories such as trauma in revolutionary historiography, see Rebecca Spang, "Paradigms and Paranoia: How Modern is the French Revolution?," *American Historical Review* 108.1 (February 2003).

5. J. Hoberman, "Spielberg's Oskar: *Schindler's List* Directed by Steven Spielberg," *Village Voice*, December 21, 1993, p. 63. Quoted in Miriam Bratu Hansen, "*Schindler's List* Is Not *Shoah*: The Second Commandment, Popular Modernism, and Public Memory," *Critical Inquiry* 22 (Winter 1996), p. 297.

6. I take the phrase "materiality of communication" from Hans Ulrich Gumbrecht and K. Ludwig Pfeiffer (eds.), *Materialities of Communication* (Stanford: Stanford University Press, 1994).

7. Antoine-Louis de Saint-Just, *Oeuvres complètes* (Paris: Gallimard, 2004), p. 642.

8. Jean-Jacques Rousseau, "Political Economy," in *The Social Contract and Other Later Political Writings*, trans. Victor Gourevitch (Cambridge: Cambridge University Press, 1997), p. 26, translation modified.

9. Jean-Jacques Rousseau, "Fragments politiques," in *Du contrat social: Précédé de Discours sur l'économie et de Du Contrat social Première version et suivi de Fragments politiques*, ed. Robert Derathé (Paris: Gallimard, 1964), p. 315.

10. [Marie Jean Antoine Nicolas Caritat de Condorcet], *L'Assemblée Nationale, aux Français* (Paris: Imprimerie Nationale, n.d. [February 16, 1792]), p. 9.

11. The failure to compile a national directory of functionaries was acknowledged in a decree issued by the Committee of Public Safety on 7 Germinal Year II (March 27, 1794). See François Alphonse Aulard, *Recueil des*

actes du Comité de Salut public avec la correspondance officielle des représentants en mission et le registre du Conseil exécutif provisoire, 28 vols. (Paris: Imprimerie Nationale, 1889–1951), vol. 12, p. 211.

12. The text of the decree is in Paul Mantouchet, *Le gouvernement révolutionnaire (10 Août 1792–4 Brumaire an IV)* (Paris: Edouard Cornely, 1912), p. 173.

13. Archives Nationales. AF II 23A, doss. 180, item 10, dated July 4 [1793].

14. These numbers are calculated from the Committee of Public Safety's payroll records, Archives Nationales, AF II 23B, doss. 191B. For evidence of the failure to collect the *certificats de civisme*, see AF II 23A, doss. 181, item 27, "Tableau des Secrétaires-Commis du Comité du Salut public de la Convention Nationale." The last entry is dated 21 Nivôse (January 10, 1794).

15. The law is reprinted in Aulard, *Recueil des actes*, vol. 9, pp. 149–60.

16. Archives Nationales, AF II 65, doss. 438, item 11, "Bases de l'organisation du bureau de la surveillance de l'exécution des lois, Comité de Salut Public." The chart is also reprinted in Augustin Cochin and Charles Charpentier, *Les actes du gouvernement révolutionnaire (23 aout 1793–27 juillet 1794)*, 3 vols. (Paris: Société d'histoire contemporaine, 1920–1937), vol. 1, pp. 550–51.

17. On these trials, see Baczko, *Comment sortir de la Terreur*, chapter 3, as well as Patrice Guennifey, *La politique de la Terreur: Essai sur la violence révolutionnaire, 1789–1794* (Paris: Fayard, 2000), pp. 130–32. The number of witnesses at Carrier's trial is provided by Jacques Dupâquier, "Le procès de Carrier," in Michelle Vovelle (ed.), *Le tournant de l'an III: Réaction et Terreur blanche dans la France révolutionnaire* (Paris: Éditions du CTHS, 1997), p. 31.

18. Jean-Baptiste-Pierre Saladin, *Rapport au nom de la Commission des vingt-un* (Paris: Rondonneau et Baudouin, 28 Ventôse Year III), p. 5. Vadier, former president of the Committee of General Security, was also accused, but went into hiding before the trial and was rarely mentioned in the debates.

19. See Arne Ording, *Le bureau de police du Comité de Salut Public: Étude sur la Terreur* (Oslo: Jacob Dybwad, 1930). The book, the only monograph on the General Police Bureau, originated as a dissertation supervised by the Robespierrist historian Albert Mathiez; it strains unconvincingly to exonerate Robespierre of any responsibility for the bureau's activities.

20. Archives Nationales, F7 4437, entry dated 29 Prarial Year II (June 17, 1794).

21. J.B.R. Lindet, *Discours prononcé par Lindet sur les dénonciations portées*

contre l'ancien Comité de salut public et le rapport de la commission des 21 (Paris: Imprimerie nationale, 1795), p. 19.

22. *Ibid.*, p. 53.

23. *Réimpression de l'ancien Moniteur*, 32 vols. (Paris: Plon, 1863–1870), vol. 24, p. 47, issue dated 6 Germinal Year III (March 26, 1795). This part of the transcript differs slightly from the printed version in Lindet, *Discours*, p. 119.

24. *Le Moniteur*, vol. 24, 7 Germinal Year III (March 27, 1795), p. 50.

25. *Ibid.*

26. Ording was able to locate 121 draft decrees. Of these, 31 were either in the handwriting of a committee member other than Robespierre, Saint-Just, and Couthon or else bore the primary signature of one of those other members. Ording, *Bureau de police*, p. 92.

27. *Le Moniteur*, vol. 24, 8 Germinal Year III (March 28, 1795), p. 72.

28. Ording, *Bureau de police*, p. 47.

29. The first pamphlet appears to be lost. The second pamphlet, from which the story is reconstructed, consists largely of official correspondence between the various participants in the case. Louis-Léon-Félicité, duc de Brancas, comte de Lauraguais, *Recueil de pièces relatives au gouvernement révolutionnaire et au despotisme de ses comités avant le 9 Thermidor* (n.p., n.d., but signed "Chauny, ce 26 Pluviôse, l'an III de la République Française" [February 14, 1795]).

30. Augustin Lejeune's memoir is entitled "Conduite politique de Lejeune, natif de Soissoins, ci-devant chef des Bureaux de la Surveillance administrative et de la Police Générale, à ses Concitoyens de Soissons." The text, along with biographical information on Lejeune, is published in Alfred Bégis, "Curiosités révolutionnaires: Saint-Just et les bureaux de la police générale," in Société des Amis des Livres, *Annuaire: XVIIe année* (Paris: Les Amis des Livres, 1896).

31. Lejeune, "Conduite politique," p. 74.

32. *Ibid.*, pp. 74–77.

33. *Ibid.*, p. 77.

34. *Ibid.*, p. 78.

35. *Ibid.*, p. 79.

36. Ording questions several other details of Lejeune's account as well. See Ording, *Bureau de police*, pp. 37–39.

37. *Journal des Débats*, 5 Messidor Year X (June 23, 1802), pp. 2–3.

38. Pougin, *La Comédie Française*, pp. 161–62.

39. *Courrier des Spectacles*, 24 Germinal Year XI (April 14, 1803), cited in Pougin, *La Comédie Française*, pp. 166–69.

40. Robert Darnton, *The Great Cat Massacre and Other Episodes in French Cultural History* (New York: Vintage Books, 1985), p. 64.

41. Nicolas-Julien Liénart, *Charles, ou Mémoires historiques de M. de la Bussière, ex-employé au Comité de Salut Public, servant de suite à l'Histoire de la Révolution française, avec des notes sur les événemens extraordinaires arrivés sous le règne des Décemvirs, rédigés par M. Liénart*, 4 vols. (Paris, 1804).

42. The report is reprinted in *L'intermédiare des Chercheurs et Curieux*, June 10, 1896, p. 125.

43. Liénart, *Charles*, vol. 3, p. 92.

44. *Ibid.*, pp. 95–96.

45. *Ibid.*, p. 109.

46. *Ibid.*, p. 132.

47. François-Alphonse Aulard, untitled review of Victorien Sardou's *Thermidor*, in *La Révolution française: Revue d'histoire moderne et contemporaine*, vol. 20 (January–June 1891), pp. 187–88.

48. On the weaknesses of Aulard's editorial methods, which were nevertheless heroic, see the bibliographical essay by R. R. Palmer, "Fifty Years of the Committee of Public Safety," *Journal of Modern History* 13.3 (September 1941), pp. 376–78.

49. Archives Nationales, AF II 23B, doss. 191B. The records note that Labussière entered the Prisoners Bureau on 16 Prarial Year II (June 4, 1794).

50. The Académie française first recognized the word "bureaucracy" in the 1798 edition of its dictionary, defining it as "Power, influence of bureau chiefs and clerks in the Administration." *Dictionnaire de l'Académie française*, 5th ed. (Paris, Firmin Didot, 1798), s.v. "bureaucratie."

51. Commenting on Carnot's defense, in particular, Ken Alder has argued that it represents a founding moment of modern technocratic state in France—"something of an ur-event in the relations of science and politics in the modern era." Ken Alder, *Engineering the French Revolution: Arms and Enlightenment in France, 1763–1815* (Princeton: Princeton University Press, 1997), p. 302.

52. M. Michaud, *Biographie universelle ancienne et moderne*, 45 vols. (Paris: Madame C. Desplaces, 1843–1865), s.v. "Labussière (Charles-Hippolyte)."

53. Michaud, *Biographie universelle*, s.v. "Pillet (Fabien)."

54. Dumas's plans are mentioned in the dedicatory epistle to Jules Claretie, *Puyjoli* (Paris: E. Dentu, 1890), p. vi.

55. Claretie, *Puyjoli*, pp. 498–500.

56. On the play and the ensuing controversy, see *L'illustration théatrale* no. 38 (August 25, 1905) as well as Eugen Weber, "About *Thermidor*: The Oblique Uses of a Scandal," *French Historical Studies* 17.2 (Fall 1991). In this article, Weber argues that the decision to censor the play had less to do with its content—which he describes as "about as politically provocative as George and Ira Gershwin's *Strike up the Band*" (332)—than with contemporary parliamentary struggles connected to the Ralliement. Weber does not seem to realize, however, that Labussière was anything other than a figment of Sardou's imagination.

57. *New York Times*, January 28, 1891, p. 4.

58. Laure Flavigny (ed.), *Larousse gastronomique* (Paris: Larousse, 1996), s.v. "Thermidor."

59. For a discussion of the context, production, and reception of the film, see Nelly Kaplan, *Napoléon* (London: British Film Institute, 1995).

60. An illustrated and annotated version of the script, including the director's notes, can be found in Abel Gance, *Napoleon: Épopée cinégraphique en cinq époques. Première époque: Bonaparte* (Paris: Jacques Bertoin, 1991).

CHAPTER THREE: THE STATE OF WANT

1. See, for example, Martin Albrow, *Bureaucracy* (New York: Praeger, 1970), for a brief history of the word "bureaucracy," as well as a discussion of its emergence as a concept in the social sciences in the eighteenth and nineteenth centuries. There are also discussions of the term's uses in eighteenth-century France in Keith Michael Baker, "Science and Politics at the End of the Old Regime," in *Inventing the French Revolution: Essays on French Political Culture in the Eighteenth Century* (Cambridge: Cambridge University Press, 1990), pp. 153–66, and J. F. Bosher, *French Finances, 1770–1795: From Business to Bureaucracy* (Cambridge: Cambridge University Press, 1970).

2. On Gournay's invention of the word "bureaucracy," see Baker, "Science and Politics at the End of the Old Regime," in *Inventing the French Revolution*, p. 160.

3. Friedrich Melchior von Grimm, *Correspondance littéraire, philosophique*

et critique par Grimm, Diderot, Raynal, Meister, etc., ed. Maurice Tourneux, 16 vols. (Paris: Garnier, 1877–1882), vol. 6, p. 30.

4. Jacques Lacan, *Le séminaire. Livre V: Les formations de l'inconscient*, ed. Jacques-Alain Miller (Paris: Éditions du Seuil, 1998), p. 23.

5. Slavoj Žižek, *For They Know Not What They Do: Enjoyment as a Political Factor*, 2nd ed. (London: Verso, 2002).

6. I am relying here on the translation in Louis-Sebastien Mercier, *Panorama of Paris: Selections from Le Tableau de Paris by Louis-Sebastien Mercier*, ed. Jeremy D. Popkin (University Park, Pennsylvania State University Press, 1999), p. 172.

7. Louis-Sebastien Mercier, *Le Tableau de Paris*, 2 vols. (Paris: Mercure de France, 1994), vol. 2, pp. 137–39.

8. On Peuchet, see Keith Michael Baker, "Public Opinion as Political Invention," in *Inventing the French Revolution*, pp. 167–202, and Daniel Gordon, *Citizens without Sovereignty: Equality and Sociability in French thought, 1670–1789* (Princeton: Princeton University Press, 1994).

9. Reprinted in Guy Thuillier (ed.), *La bureaucratie en France aux XIXe et XXe siècle* (Paris: Economica, 1987), p. 50.

10. Cited in Jan Goldstein, *Console and Classify: The French Psychiatric Profession in the Nineteenth Century* (Cambridge: Cambridge University Press, 1987), p. 157.

11. Mercier's article is reprinted in Thuillier (ed.), *La bureaucratie*, pp. 51–52.

12. R.R. Palmer (ed.), *J.-B. Say: An Economist in Troubled Times*, trans. R. R. Palmer (Princeton, Princeton University Press, 1997), pp. 16–19. On Say, see Richard Whatmore, *Republicanism and the French Revolution: An Intellectual History of Jean-Baptiste Say's Political Economy* (Oxford, Oxford University Press, 2000).

13. This letter is reprinted in Jean-Baptiste Say, *Oeuvres diverses* (Paris: Guillaumin et Cie, 1848), pp. 615–19.

14. Say, *Oeuvres diverses*, p. 619.

15. Simon Critchley, *Ethics—Politics—Subjectivity: Essays on Derrida, Levinas, and Contemporary French Thought* (London: Verso, 1999), p. 230.

16. Louis Gabriel Ambroise de Bonald, *Théorie de pouvoir politique et réligieux* (1796), *in Oeuvres complètes*, 3 vols. (Paris: J.-P. Migne, 1859), vol. 1, p.

793. He adds "It's been long said that triviality is the sublime of mediocrity."

17. Mercier, reprinted in Thuillier (ed.), *La bureaucratie en France*, p. 52.

18. *Dictionnaire de l'Académie française*, 5th ed. (Paris, Firmin Didot, 1798), s.v. "bureaucratie."

19. Pierre Rosanvallon, *L'état en France de 1789 à nos jours* (Paris: Éditions du Seuil, 1990), p. 58.

20. An essential resource on bureaucratic satire in the postrevolutionary period is Anne-Marie Bijaoui-Baron, "La bureaucratie: Naissance d'un thème et d'un vocabulaire dans la littérature française," Thèse d'état, Université de Paris-Sorbonne (Paris IV), 1981. I have relied on it both for its bibliography and its critical readings. I am also greatly indebted to the analyses in William Reddy, *The Invisible Code: Honor and Sentiment in Postrevolutionary France* (Berkeley: University of California Press, 1997).

21. See Martyn Lyons, *Le triomphe du livre: Une histoire sociologique dans la France du XIXe siècle* (Paris: Promodis, 1987), as well the essays in Henri-Jean Martin et al. (eds.), *Histoire de l'édition française*, vol. 3, *Les temps des éditeurs* (Paris: Promodis, 1985).

22. François Furet, *Revolutionary France, 1770–1880*, trans. Antonia Nevill (Oxford: Blackwell, 1995), p. 273.

23. Jean Tulard, "Les épurations en 1814 et 1815," *Souvenir Napoléonien* 396 (July–August 1994). On contemporary exposés of shifting allegiances, see Alan B. Spitzer, "Malicious Memories: Restoration Politics and the Prosopography of Turncoats," *French Historical Studies* 24.1 (Winter 2001), pp. 37–61.

24. This biographical information is from Guy Thuillier, *Témoins de l'administration: de Saint-Just à Marx* (Paris, Éditions Berger-Levrault, 1967), pp. 128–29.

25. "Moeurs administratives par M. Ymbert," *Le Mercure du dix-neuvième siècle* (Paris, 1826), vol. 12, p. 173. The review is signed "V.A." in the text but attributed to the Philarète Chasles in the table of contents. See Odette-Adina Rachman in her definitive *Un periodique libéral sous la restauration: Le Mercure du XIXe siècle (avril 1823–mars 1826)* (Geneva: Éditions Slatkine, 1984), 81.

26. *Edinburgh Review, or Critical Journal*, 44.87 (June 1826), p. 173.

27. Jacques-Gilbert Ymbert, "Bureaucratie," in Thuillier (ed), *La bureaucratie*, pp. 638–39.

28. *Ibid.*, pp. 640–42.

29. Jacques-Gilbert Ymbert, *Les moeurs administratives, pour faire suite aux observations sur les moeurs et les usages français au commencement du XIXe siècle*, 2 vols. (Paris: Ladvocat, 1825), vol. 1, pp. i–iii.

30. *Ibid.*, pp. 10–12.

31. *Ibid.*, p. 12.

32. *Ibid.*, pp. 228–29.

33. *Ibid.*, p. 229.

34. *Ibid.*, vol. 2, pp. 192–93.

35. *Ibid.*, vol. 2, pp. 194–95.

36. On the novel's composition and publishing history, see the excellent critical apparatus in Honoré de Balzac, *Les employés*, ed. Anne-Marie Meininger (Paris: Gallimard/Folio, 1985). Also useful is Mary W. Scott, "Variations between the First and the Final Edition of Balzac's 'Les Employés'," *Modern Philolog* 23.3 (February 1926), pp. 315–36. A translation can be found in Honoré de Balzac, *The Bureaucrats*, trans. Charles Foulkes (Evanston: Northwestern University Press, 1993), with an suggestive introductory essay by Marco Diani. However, this translation is marred by occasional historical flaws. For example, in a discussion of the history of credit, the translator has rendered an allusion to "Law," i.e. John Law, as "the law." The translation also mistakenly identifies itself as based on the 1838 edition of the text, although it seems almost certainly to be based on Meininger's complete edition.

37. Mary Gluck, *Popular Bohemia: Modernism and Urban Culture in Nineteenth-Century Paris* (Cambridge, MA: Harvard University Press, 2005), p. 85.

38. Balzac, *Les employés*, pp. 83 and 77. Translations are my own, though I have consulted Balzac, *The Bureaucrats*. See note 36 above.

39. Balzac, *Les employés*, p. 45.

40. *Ibid.*, p. 48.

41. See Meininger's description of the manuscripts in Balzac, *Les employés*, p. 307.

42. Balzac, *Les employés*, p. 43.

43. *Ibid.*, p. 54.

44. *Ibid.*, p. 36.

45. *Ibid.*, p. 43.

46. *Ibid.*, p. 108.

47. *Ibid.*, p. 105.

48. *Ibid.*, p. 132.

49. *Ibid.*, pp. 141–42.

50. *Ibid.*, p. 143.

51. *Ibid.*, p. 219.

52. *Ibid.*, p. 252.

53. *Ibid.*, p. 272.

54. *Dictionnaire de l'Académie française*, 6th ed. (Paris: Firmin Didot, 1835), s.v. "bureaucratie."

55. François Guizot, *Des moyens de gouvernement et d'opposition dans l'état actuel en France* (1821; Paris: Belin, 1988), p. 126.

56. Françoise Mélonio points to the importance of these cases in his early intellectual development, in *Tocqueville and the French*, trans. Beth G. Raps (Charlottesville: University Press of Virginia, 1998), p. 9.

57. Alexis de Tocqueville, *Democracy in America*, trans. George Lawrence (New York: HarperPerennial, 1988), pp. 92–93.

58. *Ibid.*, p. 208.

59. *Ibid.*, pp. 207–208.

60. *Ibid.*, p. 216.

61. *Ibid.*, pp. 217–18.

62. *Ibid.*, p. 633.

63. On the departmental councils, see Maurice Block, *Dictionnaire de l'administration française*, 2nd ed. (Paris: Berger-Levrault, 1877) and Isser Woloch, *The New Regime: Transformations of the French Civic Order, 1789–1820s* (New York: Norton, 1994). The only study specifically dedicated to Tocqueville's years on the Conseil Général de la Manche is by Edmond L'Hommedé, *Un départment français sous la monarchy de juillet: Le Conseil Général de la Manche et Alexis de Tocqueville* (Paris: Boivin, 1933). See also the introduction to volume 10, *Correspondance et écrits locaux* of Alexis de Tocqueville, *Oeuvres complètes*, ed. J.-P Mayer, 18 vols. (Paris: Gallimard, 1951–1986).

64. André Jardin, *Tocqueville: A Biography*, trans. Lydia Davis (New York: Farrar Straus Giroux, 1988), pp. 382–83.

65. Tocqueville, *Oeuvres complètes*, vol. 10, p. 317.

66. *Ibid.*, p. 186.

67. The biographical information is provided by the editor in *ibid.*, vol. 16, p. 185.

68. *Ibid.*, p. 188.

69. *Ibid.*, pp. 188–89.

70. *Ibid.*, pp. 197–98.

71. Hayden White, *Metahistory: The Historical Imagination in Nineteenth-Century Europe* (Baltimore: Johns Hopkins Press, 1973), pp. 193–94.

72. François Furet and Françoise Mélonio, "Introduction," in Alexis de Tocqueville, *The Old Regime and the Revolution*, ed. François Furet and Françoise Mélonio. trans. Alan S. Kahan (Chicago: University of Chicago Press, 1998), p. 7.

73. Tocqueville, *The Old Regime*, p. 138. Here, as elsewhere, I have modified the translation by referring to Tocqueville, *Oeuvres complètes*, vol. 2.

74. Tocqueville, *The Old Regime*, p. 139.

75. *Ibid.*, p. 139.

76. *Ibid.*, p. 139.

77. *Ibid.*, p. 145.

78. Pierre Larousse, *Grand dictionnaire universel du XIXe siècle*, 17 vols. (Paris: Administration du Grand Dictionnaire Universel, 1866–1877), s.v. "bureaucratie." The second volume, containing this article, was published in 1867. Although it is unsigned, its tone and argument suggest that it was written by Larousse himself.

79. *Ibid.*

80. Charles de Secondat, baron de Montesquieu, *The Spirit of the Laws*, ed. and trans. Anne Cohler et al. (Cambridge: Cambridge University Press, 1989), pp. 156–57.

81. Michel Foucault, *Abnormal: Lectures at the Collège de France, 1974–1975*, ed. Valerio Marchetti and Antonella Salomoni, trans. Graham Burchell (New York: Picador, 2003), pp. 12–13.

CHAPTER FOUR: THE BUREAUCRATIC MEDIUM

1. Karl Marx and Friedrich Engels, *The German Ideology*, in *Collected Works*, 50 vols. (New York: International Publishers, 1975–2004), vol. 5, p. 27, henceforward abbreviated *MECW*.

2. John Toews, *Hegelianism: The Path Toward Dialectical Humanism, 1805–1841* (Cambridge: Cambridge University Press, 1980), p. 203.

3. Quoted in David McLellan, *Karl Marx: His Life and Thought* (New York:

Harper and Row, 1973), p. 47.

4. Bruno Latour, "Visualization and Cognition: Drawing Things Together," in Michael Lynch and Steve Woolgar (eds.), *Representation in Scientific Practice* (Cambridge, MA: The MIT Press, 1990), p. 29.

5. Unsigned [Karl Marx], "Proceedings of the Sixth Rhine Province Assembly," *Rheinische Zeitung*, May 5, 1842, *MECW*, vol. 1, p. 132.

6. Andrew Piper, *Dreaming in Books: The Making of the Bibliographic Imagination in the Romantic Age* (Chicago: University of Chicago Press, 2009).

7. Marx, "Proceedings," *MECW*, vol. 1, p. 134.

8. *Ibid.*, pp. 134–35.

9. *Ibid.*.

10. Wai Chee Dimock, "Class, Gender, and a History of Metonymy," in Wai Chee Dimock and Michael Gilmore (eds.), *Rethinking Class: Literary Studies and Social Formations* (New York: Columbia University Press,), pp. 57–106.

11. "The chief defect of all hitherto existing materialism (that of Feuerbach included) is that things, reality, sensuousness are conceived only in the form of the *object, or of contemplation*, but not as *sensuous human activity, practice*, not subjectively." Marx, "Theses on Feuerbach" (1845), *MECW*, vol. 5, p. 3.

12. Karl Marx, "Justification of the Correspondent from the Mosel," *Rheinische Zeitung* no. 17, January 17, 1843, *MECW*, vol. 1, p. 336.

13. *Ibid.*, p. 346

14. *Ibid.*, p. 343.

15. *Ibid.*

16. *Ibid.*, pp. 344–45.

17. *Ibid.*

18. *Ibid.*, pp. 348–49.

19. *Ibid.*, p. 349.

20. Pierre-Marc de Biasi, "Le papier, fragile support de l'essentiel," *Les Cahiers de médiologie* 4 (1997), pp. 7–17.

21. This metaphor has been well studied by historians of science and technology. See, for example, Otto Mayr, *Authority, Liberty, and Automatic Machinery in Early Modern Europe* (Baltimore: Johns Hopkins University Press, 1986) and Jon Agar, *The Government Machine: A Revolutionary History of the Computer* (Cambridge, MA: The MIT Press, 2003).

22. Karl Marx, "Critique of Hegel's Doctrine of the State (§§261–313)," in

Early Writings, trans. Rodney Livingstone and Gregor Benton (London: Penguin / New Left Review, 1975), pp. 99 and 105.

23. G. W. F. Hegel, *Elements of the Philosophy of Right*, trans. H. B. Nisbet (Cambridge: Cambridge University Press, 1991), p. 237 (§205).

24. Marx, "Critique of Hegel's Doctrine of the State (§§261–313)," p. 108.

25. Bruno Kaiser (ed.), *Ex libris Karl Marx und Friedrich Engels: Schicksal und Verzeichnis einer Bibliothek* (Berlin: Dietz, 1967).

26. Marx, "Critique of Hegel's Doctrine of the State (§§261–313)," pp. 112–13.

27. *Ibid.*, pp. 114–15.

28. Marx, "Contribution to a Critique of Hegel's Philosophy of Right. Introduction," in *Early Writings*, pp. 246–57.

29. Karl Marx and Friedrich Engels, *The Communist Manifesto* (New York: Verso, 1998), p. 38.

30. Karl Marx, *The 18th Brumaire of Louis Bonaparte* (New York: International Publishers, 1963), pp. 121–22.

31. On the early reception of The Psychopathology *of Everyday Life*, see Normal Kiell, *Freud without Hindsight: Reviews of His Work, 1893–1939* (Madison: International Universities Press, 1988), ch. 6.

32. Carl Schorske, *Fin-de-Siècle Vienna: Politics and Culture* (New York: Vintage, 1981), p. 199.

33. Freud to Fliess, September 22, 1898. In Jeffrey Moussaieff Masson, ed. and trans., *The Complete Letters of Sigmund Freud to Wilhelm Fliess, 1887–1904* (Cambridge, MA: Harvard University Press, 1985), p. 325.

34. Michael Molnar, "Reading the Look," in Sander Gilman, Jutta Birmele, Jay Geller, and Valerie Greenberg (eds.), *Reading Freud's Reading* (New York: New York University Press, 1994), p. 77.

35. Sigmund Freud, *The Psychopathology of Everyday Life* (1901b), in *The Standard Edition of the Complete Psychological Works of Sigmund Freud*, ed. and trans. James Strachey, 24 vols. (London: Hogarth, 1953–1973), vol. 6, p. 3.

36. *Ibid.*, p. 279.

37. *Bulletin de la Société française de Philosophe*, meeting of February 23, 1957, p. 98.

38. Lacan's diminished use of the example is gathered from the entry under

"Signorelli" in Henry Krutzen, *Jacques Lacan: Séminaire 1952–1980: Index référentiel*, 3rd ed. revised and augmented (Paris: Economica, 2009), pp. 898–99.

39. Peter Swales, "Freud, Death, and Sexual Pleasure: On the Psychical Mechanism of Dr. Sigm. Freud," *Arc de Cercle* 1.1 (January 2003), pp. 5–74.

40. Perry Anderson, "On Sebastiano Timpanaro," *London Review of Books* 23. 9 (May 10, 2001), pp. 8–12.

41. See *New Left Review* 1.94 (November–December 1975).

42. Charles Rycroft, *Psychoanalysis and Beyond* (Chicago: University of Chicago Press, 1985), pp. 87–88.

43. Raymond Williams, *Culture and Materialism: Selected Essays* (London: Verso, 2005), p. 117.

44. Sebastiano Timpanaro, *The Freudian Slip: Psychoanalysis and Textual Criticism*, trans. Kate Soper (London: NLB, 1975), pp. 143 and 21–22.

45. As recounted in Joan W. Scott, "Fantasy Echo: History and the Construction of Identity," *Critical Inquiry* 27.2 (Winter 2001), pp. 284–304. These days, computers have automated these mistakes, as when Microsoft Word turns "Heidegger" into "Headgear."

46. Paul Saenger, *Space between Words: The Origins of Silent Reading* (Stanford: Stanford University Press, 1997), p. 29. Research in cognitive science has called this hypothesis into question, however. See, for example, Kevin D. Wilson and James M. Taylor, "Letters, Not Words, Are Processed Holistically," *Perception* 38.10 (2009), pp. 1572–74.

47. Timpanaro, *Freudian Slip*, p. 69.

48. *Ibid.*

49. *Ibid.*, pp. 70–71.

50. *Ibid.*, p. 40.

51. *Ibid.*, pp. 95 and 224.

52. Sigmund Freud to Martha Bernays, July 23, 1882, in Ernst L. Freud (ed.), *The Letters of Sigmund Freud, 1873–1939* (London: Hogarth Press, 1961), p. 18.

53. Freud, *The Psychopathology of Everyday Life*, *Standard Edition*, vol. 6, p 119.

54. *Ibid.*

55. *Ibid.*, pp. 119–20.

56. Sigmund Freud, *On Dreams* (1901a), *Standard Edition*, vol. 5, p. 671.

57. Didier Anzieu, *Freud's Self-Analysis*, trans. Peter Graham (London: Hogarth Press and the Institute of Psycho-analysis, 1986), p. 542.

58. Freud, *The Psychopathology of Everyday Life*, *Standard Edition*, p. 119 n. 5.

59. Timpanaro, *Freudian Slip*, p. 16.

60. Bruno Latour, "Why Has Critique Run Out of Steam? From Matters of Fact to Matters of Concern," *Critical Inquiry* 30.2 (Winter 2004), pp. 225–48.

61. Roland Barthes, "An Almost Obsessive Relation to Writing Instruments," interview originally published in *Le Monde*, September 27, 1973. Reprinted in Roland Barthes, *The Grain of the Voice: Interviews, 1962–1980*, trans. Linda Coverdale (New York: Hill and Wang, 1985), p. 177.

62. *Ibid.*, p. 180.

63. Jacques Le Goff, "Barthes administrateur," *Communications* 36 (1982), p. 45.

64. *Ibid.*, p. 46.

65. *Ibid.*, p. 48.

66. Barthes, "An Almost Obsessive Relation to Writing Instruments," p. 177.

67. Sándor Ferenczi, "The Adaptation of the Family to the Child," in *Final Contributions to the Problems and Methods of Psychoanalysis*, ed. Michael Balint (New York: Basic Books, 1955), p. 70.

68. Roland Barthes, "Écrire," in *Oeuvres complètes*, ed. Eric Marty, 5 vols. (Paris: Seuil, 2002), vol. 4, pp. 422–23. Originally published as the preface to Roger Druet and Herman Grégoire, *La civilisation de l'écriture* (Paris: Fayard / Dessain et Tolra, 1976).

CONCLUSION: THE WISH-UTENSIL

1. *Archives parlementaires*, 2nd series, 127 vols. (Paris: Librairie administrative de P. Dupont, 1879–1913), vol. 1, p. 230 (Session of 28 Pluviôse, Year VIII).

2. The classic text is Abigail J. Sellen and Richard H. R. Harper, *The Myth of the Paperless Office* (Cambridge, MA: The MIT Press, 2002).

3. Ernst Bloch, *The Principle of Hope*, 3 vols., trans. Neville Plaice, Stephen Plaice, and Paul Knight (Cambridge, MA: The MIT Press, 1995), vol. 1, pp. 355–57.

4. I am aware of two slightly different versions of this film: one obtained from the IBM archives and another posted on YouTube by the Henson

Company: http://www.youtube.com/watch?v=_IZw2CoYztk. The Henson version includes the opening montage; the IBM version doesn't.

5. Thomas Haigh, "Remembering the Office of the Future: The Origins of Word Processing and Office Automation," *IEEE Annals of the History of Computing* (October–December 2006), pp. 6–31.

6. Charles Dickens, "Administrative Reform: Theory Royal, Drury Lane, Wednesday, June 26, 1855," in *Speeches Literary and Social* (London: John Camden Hotten, 1870), pp. 132–33.

7. See Edward Eigen, "On the Record: J. M. W. Turner's Studies for the Burning of the Houses of Parliament and Other Uncertain Bequests to History," *Grey Room* 31 (Spring 2008), pp. 68–89.

8. For a history of this experience, we now have Ann M. Blair, *Too Much to Know: Managing Scholarly Information before the Modern Age* (New Haven: Yale University Press, 2010).

Index

Zone Books series design by Bruce Mau
Typesetting by Meighan Gale
Image placement and production by Julie Fry
Printed and bound by Thompson-Shore